ISSUES OF LIFE
Answered
FROM THE BIBLE

CLARENCE SEXTON

CROWN
CHRISTIAN
PUBLICATIONS
Royal Reading

ISSUES OF LIFE
Answered
FROM THE BIBLE

CLARENCE SEXTON

SECOND EDITION
COPYRIGHT
APRIL 2005

CROWN
CHRISTIAN
PUBLICATIONS
Royal Reading

PILLAR AND GROUND OF THE TRUTH

CHURCH PLANTING AND SUNDAY SCHOOL SERIES

ISSUES OF LIFE ANSWERED FROM THE BIBLE

Copyright © 2005

Crown Christian Publications

Powell, Tennessee 37849

ISBN: 1-58981-130-5

Layout and design by Stephen Troell & Joshua Tangeman
Colorization contribution by Randy Honeycutt

Printed in the United States of America

Dedication

*T*his book is affectionately dedicated to the young people of the Temple Baptist Academy and the wonderful staff and faculty of this Christian school. May these children of the *"generation to come"* walk in the truth of God's Word.

Clarence Sexton

Acts 5:42

Introduction

As believers in the Christian faith, our lives should be characterized by Christlikeness. We are to be people of conviction and compassion. Let us stand strong for the Lord Jesus Christ and stand with compassion for the souls of men.

Clarence Sexton

Acts 5:42

Contents

CAN ETERNAL LIFE BE A PRESENT POSSESSION?

t is no accident that we live in this present hour; this is the time God chose for us. We have a heavenly assignment. God knew when we would be alive and when we would have the responsibility to serve Him. He knew when we would be equipped to do the things He has for us to do. All of this is in the Lord's plan for our lives.

The only sure foundation for life is the Word of God, and the Lord employs a number of teaching methods in teaching us His Word. One of His teaching methods is the method of repetition. Another is teaching by example. There are certain things that are repeated over and over. There are certain examples lifted up for us—good examples and bad examples —things we are to do and things we are not to do.

We need a strong doctrinal foundation. We need churches that provide strong doctrinal teaching and preaching. One of the essential truths for our lives is the truth of eternal life.

We Have Eternal Life

The Bible says in I John 5:11-13,

> *And this is the record, that God hath given to us eternal life, and this life is in his Son. He that hath the Son hath life; and he that hath not the Son of God hath not life. These things have I written unto you that believe on the name of the Son of God; that ye may know that ye have eternal life, and that ye may believe on the name of the Son of God.*

Make note of the expression found in verse eleven and again in verse thirteen, *"eternal life."* For those of us who have placed our faith in Christ alone for our salvation, eternal life is our present possession.

There is a great deal of confusion about this subject. Baptists like to use the expression, "Once saved, always saved." Though I am a Baptist by conviction, I try not to use this expression. I think people sometimes say this with well-meaning intentions, thinking that they are basing this expression on some clear Bible teaching. But there is a stronger, better way to say it; that is to say it in the language of Scripture. If you mean by "once saved, always saved" that people who call themselves Christians can do as they please, you are using it in the wrong sense. Let us use a Bible term. If you mean by this that God saves us and

The only sure foundation for life is the Word of God.

keeps us saved, let us use the strong language of the Bible and call it what God calls it. He calls it *"eternal life."*

Around funeral homes and during funeral services, the people who work in these places try everything they can to take the edge off death. They say and do kind things. At the cemetery, they place a piece of grass-like carpet on the ground to hide the dirt and mud. They carry lovely flowers to the cemetery and place them around the grave plot so you do not have to look at an empty hole where the body of a loved one will be lowered into the ground. They use certain language. Hardly ever will they use the word *death*. They call it the "passing" of a loved one or the "homegoing" of a loved one.

Once we understand this clear teaching of the present possession of eternal life, we can have great joy in knowing that we are never going to be separated from the Lord Jesus Christ.

Many times, on printed material at the funeral home, you will see the name of the person and the date he died. Where the date of death is given is the statement, "Entered eternal life." For example, if the date of death were January 30, 2003, it would read, "Entered eternal life, January 30, 2003." But if that particular person were a Christian, he did not enter eternal life the day he died. He entered eternal life the day he trusted Jesus Christ as his personal Savior.

The Bible says in I John 5:13, *"These things have I written unto you that believe on the name of the Son of God; that ye may know that ye have eternal life, and that ye may believe on the name of the Son of God."* This is not a future promise. It is a present possession. Once we understand this clear teaching of the present possession of eternal life, we can have great joy in knowing that we are never going to be separated from the Lord Jesus Christ. He said Himself in John 10:27-29,

> *My sheep hear my voice, and I know them, and they follow me: and I give unto them eternal life; and they shall never perish, neither shall any man pluck them out of my hand. My Father, which gave them me, is greater than all; and no man is able to pluck them out of my Father's hand.*

Is it dangerous to teach people that they have eternal life? Perhaps I should ask, "Is it dangerous to teach people the truth?" No, it is liberating to teach people the truth. If it is misunderstood and misguided, people can twist this doctrine into something that it is not. But I praise God that my present possession as a Christian is eternal life.

We Have an Eternal God

Think about eternity. The Bible says in Deuteronomy 33:27, *"The eternal God is thy refuge, and underneath are the everlasting arms: and he shall thrust out the enemy from before thee; and shall say, Destroy them."* The Bible says we have an eternal God.

We Have an Eternal Power

In Romans 1:20, the Bible speaks of eternal power. The verse says, *"For the invisible things of him from the creation of the world are clearly seen, being understood by the things that are made, even his eternal power and Godhead; so that they are without excuse."* Our God has eternal power.

We Have an Eternal House

The Word of God teaches in II Corinthians that we have an eternal house. The Bible says in II Corinthians 5:1, *"For we know that if our earthly house of this tabernacle were dissolved, we have a building of God, an house not made with hands, eternal in the heavens."* We have an eternal house in heaven. It is not going to fade away or dissolve. Because I have entered into God's family, I am going to live forever in God's house.

My family lives in my house. My boys lived there when they were growing up. My wife and I live there now. It is my house. I am a part of the family. My family lives in my house. It is that simple. If we are a part of God's family, we are going to live in God's house.

We Have an Eternal Purpose

In Ephesians chapter three, God says we have an eternal purpose. The Bible says in verses ten and eleven,

> *To the intent that now unto the principalities and powers in heavenly places might be known by the church the manifold wisdom of God, according to the eternal purpose which he purposed in Christ Jesus our Lord.*

God has an eternal purpose. I am very grateful that I have been allowed to enter into God's eternal purpose. This is tremendously encouraging to me. I have a part in what our eternal God is doing by His eternal power. As I look forward to my eternal house, I am laboring in God's eternal purpose.

We Are Headed for an Eternal Glory

In I Peter chapter five, we find that we are headed for an eternal glory. We are sharing in that glory now. The Bible says in verse ten, *"But the God of all grace, who hath called us unto his eternal glory by Christ Jesus, after that ye have suffered a while, make you perfect, stablish, strengthen, settle you."* We have an eternal glory that never passes away.

There Is an Eternal Fire

In the seventh verse of the book of Jude, God tells us about an eternal fire. The Bible says, *"Even as Sodom and Gomorrha, and the cities about them in like manner, giving themselves over to fornication, and going after strange flesh, are set forth for an example, suffering the vengeance of eternal fire."*

Let us go back where we started, where the Bible speaks of eternal life. In the Gospel according to John, the Bible says in

> *Eternal life is not a future promise; it is a present possession.*

chapter three, verse thirty-six, *"He that believeth on the Son hath everlasting life..."* The Bible says he *"hath"* everlasting life. This is not something he is going to get. It is something he presently possesses. The verse concludes, *"...and he that believeth not the Son shall not see life; but the wrath of God abideth on him."* God says clearly in John 3:36 that, at this present moment, every believer has everlasting life.

As a believer in Jesus Christ, imagine that something happened to you and you died while you were doing something you should not be doing. This does not change the fact that you have eternal life, that you have entered into everlasting life. I entered eternal life the moment I asked God to forgive my sin and by faith trusted Christ as my Savior. If it is *eternal* life, that means it is *eternal*. If it is *everlasting* life, that means it is *everlasting*.

Nothing can take it from me! I have it as a present possession. Eternal life is not a future promise; it is a present possession.

In John 5:24 the Lord Jesus says, *"Verily, verily, I say unto you, He that heareth my word, and believeth on him that sent me, hath everlasting life, and shall not come into condemnation; but is passed from death unto life."* I have eternal life at this moment. It is a present possession.

If you believe this is a dangerous doctrine, I want to tell you why it is not. If you believe you can tell someone who is saved that he has eternal life and this gives him the privilege to live any way he pleases, even in a way that is disgraceful to God, I want to show you some things from the Bible that will help you. There is clear teaching from God's Word as to why this is not a dangerous doctrine but a most blessed truth from God's Word.

WE ARE NEW CREATURES

The natural mind thinks a certain way—the natural way. It does not consider spiritual things. When a person comes to Jesus Christ and trusts Him as Savior, he becomes a new creature in Christ Jesus. The Bible says in II Corinthians 5:17, *"Therefore if any man be in Christ, he is a new creature: old things are passed away; behold, all things are become new."*

I have a witness; I have the testimony of the Holy Spirit within me that I am a new creature. There are things that I did not desire to do that I now desire to do. There are things I once desired to do, but now I have no desire to do. Who changed all that? God did, when He came to abide in me. I am a new creature. There are habits that can be broken by the eternal power of our God who dwells in each of His children. We are new creatures.

I have known people who had no desire to come to church, but once God saved them, they wanted to be with God's people, hear God's Word, and be taught the things of God. They are new creatures.

> *When a person comes to Jesus Christ and trusts Him as Savior, he becomes a new creature in Christ Jesus.*

People have said, "I can't live that." But they have found that Christ enables them to live whatever "that" is, once they have come to trust Jesus Christ as Savior.

God has changed my life. When I do something I should not do, the Spirit of God convicts me of it and I want to be right with God about the matter because I am a new creature.

WE HAVE A NEW MOTIVE

In II Corinthians 5:14 the Bible says, *"For the love of Christ constraineth us; because we thus judge, that if one died for all, then were all dead."* Our new motive is the love of Christ.

As I consider what the Lord Jesus did for me, I want to serve Him, live for Him, love Him, adore Him, and do as He pleases. As the Christian song says, "I've already decided His will is my choice." When I find out what God wants, I have already decided that whatever He wants is what I want to do because I am constrained by a new motive. It is the love of Christ.

WE HAVE A NEW FATHER

Another good reason this is a great doctrinal truth is that we have a new Father. We cannot do as we please because our Father will not allow us to get by with it. The natural man does not consider this. The Bible says in Hebrews 12:1-11,

> *Wherefore seeing we also are compassed about with so great a cloud of witnesses, let us lay aside every weight, and the sin which doth so easily beset us, and let us run with patience the race that is set before us, looking unto Jesus the author and finisher of our faith; who for the joy that was set before him endured the cross, despising the shame, and is set down at the right hand of the throne of God. For consider him that endured such contradiction of sinners against himself, lest ye be wearied and faint in your minds. Ye have not yet resisted unto blood, striving against sin. And ye have forgotten the exhortation which speaketh unto you as unto children, My son, despise not thou the chastening of the Lord, nor faint when thou art rebuked of him: for whom the Lord loveth he chasteneth, and scourgeth every son whom he receiveth. If ye endure chastening, God dealeth with you as with sons; for what son is he whom the father chasteneth not? But if ye be without chastisement, whereof all are partakers, then are ye bastards, and not sons. Furthermore we have*

Our new motive is the love of Christ.

*had fathers of our flesh which corrected us, and
we gave them reverence: shall we not much
rather be in subjection unto the Father of spirits,
and live? For they verily for a few days chastened
us after their own pleasure; but he for our profit,
that we might be partakers of his holiness. Now
no chastening for the present seemeth to be
joyous, but grievous: nevertheless afterward it
yieldeth the peaceable fruit of righteousness unto
them which are exercised thereby.*

We have a new Father who will deal with His children. He
will chasten us. We cannot sin and get by with it.

If you are standing somewhere watching a group of children
play and you see them getting into something they should not
get into, if your children are in that group, you do not discipline
every child that is involved, but you get your children and take
care of your children. As a matter of fact, you may call your
children's names. You may call their full names. You know when
they need to be disciplined. The point I am making is that a
father takes care of his own children.

It is possible that a man who is unsaved and a man who is
saved can be involved in the very same evil, awful thing. The
man who is not a Christian may seem to get by with it and never
have anything happen to him. Do you know why? He may seem
to get by with it for now, but he is going to spend an eternity in
hell if he does not trust Christ as Savior. The fellow who is a
Christian can do the same evil, awful thing, but God is going to
chasten him because he is in God's family.

WE HAVE A NEW JUDGMENT

If you die without Christ, you are going to stand before God at the Great White Throne Judgment. The Christian will not be judged for his sin because his sin was judged in the body of Christ on the cross.

Mr. Spafford had it right when he wrote the hymn, "It Is Well With My Soul." One of the verses states, "My sin, not in part, but the whole, is nailed to the cross, and I bear it no more."

Those who are saved are going to the judgment seat of Christ. We will not be judged there for our sin; our sin was judged on the cross. But we are going to be judged for our works. This is a serious matter. Someone may say, "I don't care, just as long as I get to heaven." This is the wrong attitude to have. If your house was on fire, would you run out of it and say, "I don't care who suffers, who gets caught in the flames, just so I get out"? Would you treat physical life that way? Of course not! Think of others who need to know Christ as Savior to escape the fires of hell.

The Word of God says in I Corinthians 3:11-15,

> *For other foundation can no man lay than that is laid, which is Jesus Christ. Now if any man build upon this foundation gold, silver, precious stones, wood, hay, stubble; every man's work shall be made manifest: for the day shall declare it, because it shall be revealed by fire; and the fire shall try every man's work of what sort it is. If any man's work abide which he hath built thereupon, he shall receive a reward. If any man's work shall be burned, he shall suffer loss: but he himself shall be saved; yet so as by fire.*

We have eternal life. This is not a dangerous doctrine. I am going to meet the Lord, and my works are going to be judged for my motives—not just what I did, but why I did it.

> *There is an abiding satisfaction when we do what we do for Christ.*

So much of our time is given to be seen of men. This may bring some temporary approval, but soon the little satisfaction we glean from it will be over. There is an abiding satisfaction when we do what we do for Christ.

WE HAVE A NEW FREEDOM

Christians are free. The Bible says in Titus 2:13-14,

> *Looking for that blessed hope, and the glorious appearing of the great God and our Saviour Jesus Christ; who gave himself for us, that he might redeem us from all iniquity, and purify unto himself a peculiar people, zealous of good works.*

I am redeemed. I have a new freedom. I went through a period in my life as a young Christian when I thought that if I were to die while doing something I should not do, I would go to hell. Many Christian people live this way. When Jesus Christ paid our sin debt, how much of it did He pay? What does the Bible say? He paid it all! All of our sins were future when Christ died on the cross.

Thank God for the sinless life and record of our Redeemer because this is the record God put on our account. Christ was judged for my sin. The Bible says in II Corinthians 5:21 that He was made *"to be sin for us, who knew no sin; that we might be made the righteousness of God in him."* Christ was judged for all my sin on the cross.

You may say, "You have to *pay* for your sins!" I think I know what people mean by that term, but it is not correct. We do not *pay* for our sins; Christ paid for our sins. We are chastened for our sins. If you call that payment, it is not really the correct way to express it because the wages of sin is death—separation from God forever.

Once you have trusted Christ as Savior, God counts your sin debt paid because Jesus Christ tasted death for every man on the cross. He imputes Christ's righteousness to your account. He puts on your record the pure, spotless, sinless life of the Son of God. When we say we are *justified*, this does not mean, "just as

All of our sins were future when Christ died on the cross.

if we had never sinned." The record says it is "just as if we had never been sinners" because Christ's record is not "just as if He had never sinned." Christ's record shows that He was never even a sinner. This is the record that is on our account in heaven.

We have a new freedom. How can anyone sin against such love and such freedom? My life is not my own; it belongs to Christ. I have been conquered by Calvary.

Someone said to a saintly lady one day, "Just imagine that you are wrong about this and you got into sin and suddenly you died in sin. What do you think about that?"

This saintly lady replied, "It would be a greater loss for God than it would be for me if I went to hell."

"What do you mean by that?"

"Yes," she said, "it would be a greater loss for God than it would be for me because of what He would lose. He would lose His honor because He has promised that I have eternal life and nothing can take that away."

> *Those who know Christ as Savior do not enter eternal life when they die; they enter eternal life when they trust the Lord Jesus as Savior.*

Out of a grateful heart, we should rejoice that we have eternal life if we are saved. My darling mother is in heaven. She entered eternal life when she trusted Christ as Savior, so when it came time to die, there was no parting, no pausing. Christ just took her.

Those who know Christ as Savior do not enter eternal life when they die; they enter eternal life when they trust the Lord Jesus as Savior. This is not a future promise; it is a present possession. This does not make me want to go out and live a sinful life. It moves my heart and causes me to give my life completely to the Lord Jesus.

CAN ETERNAL LIFE BE A PRESENT POSSESSION?

BIBLE MEMORY VERSES

"For God so loved the world, that he gave his only begotten Son, that whosoever believeth in him should not perish, but have everlasting life."

John 3:16

"He that believeth on the Son hath everlasting life: and he that believeth not the Son shall not see life; but the wrath of God abideth on him."

John 3:36

"Verily, verily, I say unto you, He that heareth my word, and believeth on him that sent me, hath everlasting life, and shall not come into condemnation; but is passed from death unto life."

John 5:24

"My sheep hear my voice, and I know them, and they follow me: and I give unto them eternal life; and they shall never perish, neither shall any man pluck them out of my hand. My Father, which gave them me, is greater than all; and no man is able to pluck them out of my Father's hand."

John 10:27-29

"For the which cause I also suffer these things: nevertheless I am not ashamed: for I know whom I have believed, and am persuaded that he is able to keep that which I have committed unto him against that day."

II Timothy 1:12

"Nevertheless the foundation of God standeth sure, having this seal, The Lord knoweth them that are his. And, Let every one that nameth the name of Christ depart from iniquity."

II Timothy 2:19

"In hope of eternal life, which God, that cannot lie, promised before the world began."

Titus 1:2

"And this is the record, that God hath given to us eternal life, and this life is in his Son. He that hath the Son hath life; and he that hath not the Son of God hath not life. These things have I written unto you that believe on the name of the Son of God; that ye may know that ye have eternal life, and that ye may believe on the name of the Son of God."

I John 5:11-13

Chapter Two

IS THE BIBLE THE WORD OF GOD?

he Bible is the sole authority for all we believe and teach. The Bible is a precious treasure. Is God the author? Is it a perfect Book? Is it inerrant, inspired, and infallible?

All of us believe something. Because of what we believe, we live a certain way. Our beliefs determine our behavior. If we believe the Bible, then we should be living according to the Bible. The Bible is to be read and obeyed.

WHAT OTHERS HAVE SAID ABOUT THE BIBLE

"The vigor of our spiritual life will be in exact proportion to the place held by the Bible in our life and thoughts."

– George Mueller

"Nobody ever outgrows Scripture; the book widens and deepens with our years."

— Charles Haddon Spurgeon

"In all my perplexities and distresses, the Bible has never failed to give me light and strength."

— Robert E. Lee

"I am sorry for the men who do not read the Bible every day; I wonder why they deprive themselves of the strength and of the pleasure."

— Woodrow Wilson

"I never knew all there was in the Bible until I spent those years in jail. I was constantly finding new treasures."

— John Bunyan

"The most learned, acute, and diligent student cannot, in the longest life, obtain an entire knowledge of the Bible. The more deeply he works the mine, the richer and more abundant he finds the ore."

— Sir Walter Scott

"So great is my veneration for the Bible that the earlier my children begin to read it, the more confident will be my hope that they will prove useful citizens to their country, and respectable members of society."

— John Quincy Adams

The Bible says in II Timothy 3:16-17, *"All scripture is given by inspiration of God, and is profitable for doctrine, for reproof, for correction, for instruction in righteousness: that the man of God may be perfect, throughly furnished unto all good works."*

Notice the phrase, *"All scripture is given by inspiration of God."* This means that the Bible is God-breathed. Since God is the author of the Bible, it is the source of authority for faith and life.

Is the Bible the Word of God? There is only one reliable source in all the world to tell me who God is and what God is like. That source is the Bible. The Bible is God's revelation of Himself and of His Word to man. The Bible tells us who He is. The Bible shows us what He is like as we see the Person of the Lord Jesus Christ coming from heaven's glory, being born of a virgin in Bethlehem's manger, living a sinless life, dying for our sins on Calvary, being buried in a borrowed tomb, and coming forth from the grave alive forevermore.

> *The Bible is God's revelation of Himself and of His Word to man.*

The Bible is the Book that tells us where we came from and why we are here. In the Bible, God does not tell us everything He knows; He tells us everything He wants us to know. The Bible is the only Book that tells me where I am going when I leave this earth. There are questions deeply planted in the heart of every human being that can only be adequately answered from the Bible. If the Bible is the only source for those answers, and there is a real heaven and a real hell and we are headed to one of those places; if the Bible is the Book that tells us how to get to heaven, then the Devil must hate it with more passion than we have ever imagined. Anyone who has been used of God to preach the Bible or get the Bible to people has been a person that the Devil hates.

In A.D. 303, the Roman emperor Diocletian declared that he was going to remove Christianity and the Bible from the face of the earth. He ordered that every copy of the Word of God be destroyed and every Christian killed. Two years later, he erected a monument that stated, "Christianity has been extinguished from the face of the earth."

> *There are questions deeply planted in the heart of every human being that can only be adequately answered from the Bible.*

A few years later in A.D. 312, the Roman emperor Constantine declared that the Roman empire was Christian. Of course, Constantine's declaration was not accurate, but the point is that it is impossible to remove God's Word and God's people from this earth until God gets ready to take us out.

The Bible is the Word of God. Centuries ago, a man by the name of John Wycliffe wanted the common man to read the Bible. He translated the Scriptures so that common people could read the Word of God.

During the Inquisition the Catholic church ordered that Wycliffe be killed. They hated him for putting the Bible in the hands of the people. Before they could reach him, he died. But they had such hatred for what he had done with the Word of God, getting the message to people, they ordered that his body be dug up and his corpse burned.

Do you want to know what this world would be like without the Bible? If you read Genesis 6:5, you find that God said, speaking of man, *"Every imagination of the thoughts of his heart was only evil continually."* God made a decision that the entire world would be destroyed. Adam's race had gone astray. Noah, his three sons, and their wives were the only ones in all the human race who were spared from the wrath of God.

What brought about such a condition? There was no written revelation of God and His Word. We see here the world without a Bible.

We live in a wicked world. Wickedness abounds, not because we do not have a Bible, but because we have neglected the Bible. We have purchased Bibles and put them on shelves in our homes and have not read them. We have gone through a revolution of the mind, not just in America, but all around the world.

> *Wickedness abounds, not because we do not have a Bible, but because we have neglected the Bible.*

If one generation can be removed from the Word of God, their minds can be captured by the Devil. This is exactly what we are seeing take place.

THE TESTIMONY OF THE BIBLE CONCERNING ITSELF

Consider what the Bible says of itself. In II Timothy 3:16 the Bible says, *"All scripture is given by inspiration of God."* This means it is all God-breathed.

When God breathed this Word, He chose over forty different human instruments to pen His Word over a period of 1,500 years or more. The Bible says of itself–and it is either true or it is a lie–that it is the breath of God.

In II Peter 1:21 the Bible says, *"For the prophecy came not in old time by the will of man: but holy men of God spake as they were moved by the Holy Ghost."*

The Bible says in I Corinthians 2:13, *"Which things also we speak, not in the words which man's wisdom teacheth, but which the Holy Ghost teacheth; comparing spiritual things with spiritual."*

Notice the use of this expression, *"words."* Every word of the Bible is the Word of God. That is why we should give attention to *all* Scripture. The Bible is trustworthy in all parts. The apostles used the Old Testament for preaching and teaching. The New Testament writers quoted from the Old Testament extensively. Wherever the Bible touches any subject, the statements made on that subject (biology, psychology, history) are trustworthy, but that is not the purpose of the Bible. The purpose of the Bible is clearly stated in Scripture.

The Bible says in Isaiah 40:6-8,

> *The voice said, Cry. And he said, What shall I cry? All flesh is grass, and all the goodliness thereof is as the flower of the field: the grass withereth, the flower fadeth: because the spirit of the LORD bloweth upon it: surely the people is grass. The grass withereth, the flower fadeth: but the word of our God shall stand for ever.*

The Bible says of itself that it is the Word of God. The Bible says of itself that its origin is God. If you ask for the testimony of the Bible about itself, the Bible declares that it is the Word of God.

Do you want to know the truth? It is the truth that sets men free. The truth is the Bible.

The Bible says in Psalm 119:89, *"For ever, O LORD, thy word is settled in heaven."* Before any word of the Bible was ever given to any man to pen, every word of it was settled in heaven. It is the Word of God.

My first encounter with an outspoken person who did not believe the Bible was in a Bible class in college. Can you imagine standing before a Bible class, claiming to be a Bible teacher, and saying the Bible is not the Word of God?

Before any word of the Bible was ever given to any man to pen, every word of it was settled in heaven.

It has become common for many people to say what only some college professors used to say, "The Bible is full of error," "The Bible isn't true," "The Bible is archaic, written years ago," "The Bible is not relevant."

The Bible has never changed. The Bible is the Word of God. Anyone who does not believe this is going to die and go to hell forever. I do not like saying this, but it is the truth. The Bible says in John 5:24, *"Verily, verily, I say unto you, He that heareth my word, and believeth on him that sent me, hath everlasting life, and shall not come into condemnation; but is passed from death unto life."* The only way to escape this condemnation is to hear and believe the Word of God. The Bible is the Word of God.

As Christian people, we must not forsake our position on the Bible. Stand with love and compassion. Be kind and Christlike about it. But may God help us to be uncompromising concerning what we believe about the Bible. It is the Word of God. It will never change. The testimony of the Bible concerning itself is that it is God's Word.

THE TESTIMONY OF JESUS CHRIST CONCERNING THE BIBLE

The skeptics say that they do not believe the story of Jonah and the whale as it is given in the Bible. They do not believe that a fish could swallow a man and the man could live. The Bible says that it is true.

> *May God help us to be uncompromising concerning what we believe about the Bible. It is the Word of God.*

Notice what the Lord Jesus said. If you believe that the Lord Jesus is God, coequal, coexistent, eternally existent with God the Father and God the Holy Spirit, then you will believe what Jesus Christ said. Notice what He said about the Bible in Matthew 12:38-40. The Word of God says,

> *Then certain of the scribes and of the Pharisees answered, saying, Master, we would see a sign from thee. But he answered and said unto them, An evil and adulterous generation seeketh after a sign; and there shall no sign be given to it, but the sign of the prophet Jonas: for as Jonas was three days and three nights in the whale's belly; so shall the Son of man be three days and three nights in the heart of the earth.*

Christ was talking about His death, burial, and resurrection. He compared it to the biblical account of Jonah and the whale. The Lord Jesus declared the Bible to be true.

One of my professors at the university stood and said that all that "baloney" about the creation of the world should not be believed by sensible people. He said that there was no scientific accuracy in the account given in the Bible.

Hear the testimony of the Lord Jesus in Matthew 19:3-4 concerning creation,

> *The Pharisees also came unto him, tempting him, and saying unto him, Is it lawful for a man to put away his wife for every cause? And he answered and said unto them, Have ye not read, that he which made them at the beginning made them male and female?*

The Lord Jesus Christ declared the Bible to be true. God made Adam and Eve.

Do you know more than God knows? Do you know something God does not know? Does a preacher who denies the Bible is God's Word, along with a congregation who is foolish enough to follow him, know more than the Son of God knows? We know they do not. So let us, without apology, boldly declare that we believe what the Lord Jesus Himself believes. He says the Bible is the Word of God.

Many scoff at the idea concerning the Flood in Noah's day. In Matthew 24:35-39 the Lord Jesus said,

> *Heaven and earth shall pass away, but my words shall not pass away. But of that day and hour knoweth no man, no, not the angels of heaven, but my Father only. But as the days of Noe were, so shall also the coming of the Son of man be. For as in the days that were before the flood they were eating and drinking, marrying and giving in marriage, until the day that Noe entered into the ark, and knew not until the flood*

came, and took them all away; so shall also the coming of the Son of man be.

They laughed and scoffed at the idea of a man building an ark, and now they are trying to find the ark to substantiate the Bible. You do not have to find the ark to prove the Bible is true. I believe it because God said it. But whether I believe it or not, the fact that God said it means it is true.

Jesus Christ gave the testimony that He believed the biblical account of Noah and the ark. I do not presume to know more than He knows. I think a man is a fool if he presumes to know more than God knows.

Look once again at the testimony of Jesus Christ concerning God's Word in Luke chapter twenty-four. Jesus Christ had been to Calvary to bleed and die for our sins. After His resurrection, He was walking the road to Emmaus. He made a statement to the discouraged disciples. They did not understand His death, burial, and resurrection. Luke 24:25 says, *"Then he said unto them, O fools, and slow of heart to believe all that the prophets have spoken."*

The testimony of Jesus Christ is that everything that the prophets have spoken should be believed. All of it is the Word of God.

THE TESTIMONY OF THOSE WHO HAVE TRUSTED THE LORD CONCERNING THE BIBLE

The testimony of the Bible concerning itself is that it is the Word of God. The testimony of the Lord Jesus concerning the Bible is that it is the Word of God. What about the testimony of those who have trusted the Lord?

The apostle Paul wrote in II Timothy 3:15, *"And that from a child thou hast known the holy scriptures, which are able to make thee wise unto salvation through faith which is in Christ Jesus."*

Paul said, "Timothy, I am writing to you about the Bible because it is the Bible that made you wise unto salvation. Because of the Bible, you heard about salvation in the Lord Jesus Christ."

The apostle Paul could tell you that one day on the road to Damascus when Jesus Christ met him and spoke to him, he yielded his life to Christ. It was God's Word that convicted him through the lives of those who were living for the Lord. Paul believed the Bible was the Word of God.

If you talked to Timothy, he would tell you, "When I was a boy, my mother and grandmother taught me the Bible and told me about the Lord. I became a Christian as a result of the Word of God."

Everyone who has been saved could stand and give a testimony that believing God's Word changed his life. When was the last time you heard a man say he read a math book or a chemistry book and his life was changed? We do not hear such things.

I have a brother who is thirteen months younger than I am. I prayed for my brother's salvation for nine years. He was bound by sin before he came to know Christ.

Today my brother is a preacher of the gospel, serving the Lord. He pastors a great church which he started in Southwest Florida. He could stand and testify to you, "I believe the Bible is the Word of God because the Bible broke my bonds, set me free, and changed my life."

One day I walked down the hallway with the music and youth director of the First Baptist Church in Maryville, Tennessee. He took me into a room and we sat across from the pastor. I was frightened because I knew so little about the things of God. He said to me, "I want to show you how to be saved. I want to show you from the Bible how to know the Lord as your Savior."

> *Simply understanding the Bible will not bring salvation. The message must be believed and obeyed.*

Simply understanding the Bible will not bring salvation. The message must be believed and obeyed. As we sat there together, he read the Bible to me and asked this question, "Do you believe the Bible?"

I said, "Yes, sir."

He said, "The Bible says, *'For God so loved the world, that he gave his only begotten Son, that whosoever believeth in him should not perish, but have everlasting life.'* Son, will you believe God's Word, ask God to forgive your sin, and trust Jesus Christ as your Savior?"

I want you to know that when I said, "Yes," bells did not ring; lights did not flash; I did not feel strange all over. But I took God at His Word and God kept His Word. He forgave my sin and came to live in my life, and He has never left me.

The Bible declares of itself that it is the Word of God. Jesus Christ taught that every part of the Bible is the Word of God. I can testify with others who have trusted Christ as Savior, that the Bible is truly the Word of God. Approach the Bible with faith and prayer. The Bible says in John 7:17, *"If any man will do his will, he shall know of the doctrine, whether it be of God, or whether I speak of myself."* God will make His Word known to those who are willing to obey.

IS THE BIBLE THE WORD OF GOD?

BIBLE MEMORY VERSES

"The words of the LORD are pure words: as silver tried in a furnace of earth, purified seven times. Thou shalt keep them, O LORD, thou shalt preserve them from this generation for ever."

Psalm 12:6-7

"For ever, O LORD, thy word is settled in heaven."

Psalm 119:89

"The grass withereth, the flower fadeth: but the word of our God shall stand for ever."

Isaiah 40:8

"For verily I say unto you, Till heaven and earth pass, one jot or one tittle shall in no wise pass from the law, till all be fulfilled."

Matthew 5:18

"Heaven and earth shall pass away, but my words shall not pass away."

Matthew 24:35

"Which things also we speak, not in the words which man's wisdom teacheth, but which the Holy Ghost teacheth; comparing spiritual things with spiritual."

I Corinthians 2:13

"For this cause also thank we God without ceasing, because, when ye received the word of God which ye heard of us, ye received it not as the word of men, but as it is in truth, the word of God, which effectually worketh also in you that believe."

I Thessalonians 2:13

41

"And that from a child thou hast known the holy scriptures, which are able to make thee wise unto salvation through faith which is in Christ Jesus. All scripture is given by inspiration of God, and is profitable for doctrine, for reproof, for correction, for instruction in righteousness: that the man of God may be perfect, throughly furnished unto all good works."

II Timothy 3:15-17

"For the word of God is quick, and powerful, and sharper than any twoedged sword, piercing even to the dividing asunder of soul and spirit, and of the joints and marrow, and is a discerner of the thoughts and intents of the heart."

Hebrews 4:12

"Being born again, not of corruptible seed, but of incorruptible, by the word of God, which liveth and abideth for ever."

I Peter 1:23

"Knowing this first, that no prophecy of the scripture is of any private interpretation. For the prophecy came not in old time by the will of man: but holy men of God spake as they were moved by the Holy Ghost."

II Peter 1:20-21

IS THERE A PLACE OF TORMENT?

here are times in the Bible when the Lord pulls the curtain and allows us to look into the world beyond. We know there are two real worlds. There is the world in which we live, the world in which we see things. But there is a world just as real beyond this present world in which we live. God reveals certain things about that world to us through word pictures He paints for us in the Bible.

Is there really a place of torment? Do people go there? The Bible says in Luke 16:19-31,

> *There was a certain rich man, which was clothed in purple and fine linen, and fared sumptuously every day: and there was a certain beggar named Lazarus, which was laid at his*

45

gate, full of sores, and desiring to be fed with the crumbs which fell from the rich man's table: moreover the dogs came and licked his sores. And it came to pass, that the beggar died, and was carried by the angels into Abraham's bosom: the rich man also died, and was buried; and in hell he lift up his eyes, being in torments, and seeth Abraham afar off, and Lazarus in his bosom. And he cried and said, Father Abraham, have mercy on me, and send Lazarus, that he may dip the tip of his finger in water, and cool my tongue; for I am tormented in this flame. But Abraham said, Son, remember that thou in thy lifetime receivedst thy good things, and likewise Lazarus evil things: but now he is comforted, and thou art tormented. And beside all this, between us and you there is a great gulf fixed: so that they which would pass from hence to you cannot; neither can they pass to us, that would come from thence. Then he said, I pray thee therefore, father, that thou wouldest send him to my father's house: for I have five brethren; that he may testify unto them, lest they also come into this place of torment. Abraham saith unto him, They have Moses and the prophets; let them hear them. And he said, Nay, father Abraham: but if one went unto them from the dead, they will repent. And he said unto him, If they hear not Moses and the prophets, neither will they be persuaded, though one rose from the dead.

Consider the subject taken from verse twenty-eight, *"this place of torment."* These words came from the Lord Jesus. This is the Word of God.

The Bible says in Luke 16:23, *"And in hell he lift up his eyes, being in torments."* The Bible says in Luke 16:24, *"I am tormented in this flame."* In Luke 16:25, the rich man is spoken to and the Bible says, *"Thou art tormented."* The rich man calls this place where he has gone for eternity, *"this place of torment."*

I was recently reading a story in a news magazine about an incident that took place in Saudi Arabia, in the city of Mecca. There were 750 young ladies in a girls' school. Because of their Muslim religion, the girls' bodies were completely covered. Their heads were covered. One of these Muslim girls decided that she was going to light a cigarette in a narrow hallway. Someone saw her, so to keep from being found out, she threw the cigarette into a corner where there were some old papers and went back to class.

It was not long until someone smelled the odor of smoke. The girls knew that the building was on fire. It was not an appropriate school building; it was an apartment building that had been converted somewhat into a school building in a bad part of town.

The Muslim police were outside the building because there was a strict code that stated that a man could not look at the uncovered face of any of these girls. So as the girls, in their panic, started running through the narrow hallways, many of them took off the top part of their garment so that they could breathe more easily. When they went to the doors, they found the doors were chained.

As the girls finally reached the place to get out, there were Muslim police officers who would not let them out of the building. They actually threw some of the girls back into the burning building because their faces were uncovered. The policemen knew that firemen were there to put out the fire and they did not want the firemen to see the faces of these girls. The policemen would rather that the girls burn to death in the fire than have their faces seen.

Finally, someone came and removed the policemen and allowed the girls to get out of the building. Forty of them were seriously injured, and fifteen of them were burned or trampled to death in the fire.

> *Physical death is separation from the body. Spiritual death is separation from God.*

This is a sad story about a sad world and a tragically misguided people who believe the lies of the Devil. When I think about those girls trying to run for their lives, I think of the horror of this awful circumstance. But there is something worse than that. They had been told a religious lie and believed it. The fire they went through and died in was not nearly so horrible as the place of torment they went to if they did not know the Lord Jesus as their Savior.

I do not like to think about people going to hell. God's Word is true, and the Lord Jesus said, *"I am the way, the truth, and the life: no man cometh unto the Father, but by me"* (John 14:6). God wants us to know that hell is real.

When Ted Williams, one of baseball's greats, died, his family did something unusual with his body. Dr. Stephen Morris, an advisor at the Alcore Life Extension Foundation in Arizona, reported that Ted Williams' body was taken there and packed, not in ice, but injected with a substance that keeps the blood from clotting. Then, chemical ice crystals form so as not to damage the cells. They say that people are frozen, but technically that is not correct. They are put into a container that looks like a giant thermos bottle. The temperature slowly cools down with liquid nitrogen, and the body is saved all because someone thinks, through the efforts of modern science, they might bring him back to life. It cost the family of Ted Williams $120,000 for this procedure.

I want to ask you, do you think Ted Williams is in a thermos bottle in Arizona? No, and though it is tragic, a man who would order something like that to be done has most likely never believed the truth of God's Word. I hope that he was a Christian.

I hope those girls in Saudi Arabia had heard the message of Jesus Christ and trusted Christ as Savior. But I doubt very seriously that in a world like theirs they ever heard the gospel.

Physical death is separation from the body. Spiritual death is separation from God. The Bible says in Ephesians 2:1, *"And you hath he quickened, who were dead in trespasses and sins."* In other words, every human being is stillborn spiritually. We are spiritually dead. Spiritual death means to be separated from God. To be separated from God in life means that when we are physically dead and separated from our bodies, we are going to be separated from God forever.

THE PROOF OF THIS PLACE OF TORMENT IS GIVEN TO US IN THE SCRIPTURES

The Bible teaches that there are only two places beyond this world where people go. One is heaven and the other is hell.

The Bible is our only source of information concerning hell. The Bible says in Luke 16:22-24,

> *The rich man also died, and was buried; and in hell he lift up his eyes, being in torments, and seeth Abraham afar off, and Lazarus in his bosom. And he cried and said, Father Abraham,*

have mercy on me, and send Lazarus, that he may dip the tip of his finger in water, and cool my tongue; for I am tormented in this flame.

In Matthew 13:49-50 the Bible says,

So shall it be at the end of the world: the angels shall come forth, and sever the wicked from among the just, and shall cast them into the furnace of fire: there shall be wailing and gnashing of teeth.

In Matthew 23:33, our Lord says, speaking to the religious hypocrites, *"Ye serpents, ye generation of vipers, how can ye escape the damnation of hell?"*

Matthew 25:41 says, *"Then shall he say also unto them on the left hand, Depart from me, ye cursed, into everlasting fire, prepared for the devil and his angels."*

Matthew 25:46 says, *"And these shall go away into everlasting punishment: but the righteous into life eternal."*

In Revelation 14:10 the Bible says,

The same shall drink of the wine of the wrath of God, which is poured out without mixture into the cup of his indignation; and he shall be tormented with fire and brimstone in the presence of the holy angels, and in the presence of the Lamb.

Revelation 19:20 says,

And the beast was taken, and with him the false prophet that wrought miracles before him, with which he deceived them that had received the mark of the beast, and them that worshipped his image. These both were cast alive into a lake of fire burning with brimstone.

Revelation 20:10 says, *"And the devil that deceived them was cast into the lake of fire and brimstone, where the beast and the false prophet are, and shall be tormented day and night for ever and ever."* The proof that this place of torment exists is given to us in Scripture.

There is a real place prepared for the Devil and his angels. It is a place the Bible calls Hell. There is nothing pleasant about it. There is nothing kind about it. It is a place of torment. It is a place of unending darkness, forever falling and forever dying. It is a place where no friends and family will be known, no smiles ever given, no sweet fragrances ever smelled. It is a place where no kindness is ever spoken. It is a place where no children will ever be seen. It is a horrible place, but it is a place. Just as much as Knoxville, Tennessee, is a place, there is a place called hell.

PEOPLE GO TO THIS PLACE OF TORMENT

When I read in the Bible that the Devil and his angels are cast into this place, I think, "They belong there. This is right, and I am glad the Devil gets what is coming to him." But the Bible teaches that people go to this place of torment. Every human being has been created for eternity and is either going to heaven or hell.

I do not want anyone to go to this place of torment. I believe that I am saying the same thing that God would say. His Word says that He is "not willing that any should perish, but that all should come to repentance" (II Peter 3:9). But people do go to hell.

The rich man in Luke chapter sixteen actually lived. There was a real man named Lazarus *"which was laid at his gate, full of sores, and desiring to be fed with the crumbs which fell from the rich man's table."*

Both of these men died. The Bible says in Hebrews 9:27, *"And as it is appointed unto men once to die."* Death is a possibility, but the Second Coming of Christ is a certainty. It is certain that He is coming again, but if He does not come soon, we are going through the door of death. When we go through the door of death, we are going into eternity. And untold millions are going to hell.

> *Every human being has been created for eternity and is either going to heaven or hell.*

The rich man had a family. In hell, he started talking about his family. He said, "I have five brothers." Think about growing up with five brothers. Think about the fun they had as brothers and the things they did together as children. Think about how brothers love one another and care about one another and desire to be together. But here was a man who went to a place and said, "I never want to see my brothers again! I don't want my brothers to come to this place of torment! Let someone testify to my five brethren lest they also come to this place of torment!"

There are people who have died and gone to hell whose voices we cannot hear, but they would say the same thing about their family members. They do not want their family members in this place of torment.

Many people you see every day, people you work with, people you know, people who are members of your family, are on their way to hell.

Life is so uncertain. Death can come so suddenly. No matter who you are, you need to make sure heaven is your home.

I am ashamed that we say so little about hell. I am ashamed that we preach and teach so little about hell. Preachers like me get accused of overdoing two subjects–hell and money. If there are two subjects preachers neglect, they are the subjects of hell and money. There is no doubt we should speak more about money and we should speak more about hell.

In Luke chapter sixteen, the Lord spoke about money and also about hell. He talked about investing one's money, getting people saved, and the danger of loving riches. He spoke of a man in the opening part of the chapter who called all his favors in and used his money for his personal gain. Then the Lord Jesus warned His disciples to use their money to win the lost to Christ so they could see those they won to Christ in heaven.

> *Death is a possibility, but the Second Coming of Christ is a certainty.*

Over a century ago, there lived a preacher by the name of Elbert Munsey. The Knoxville, Tennessee paper called him the most eloquent man in the south. Almost all of his preaching was on the subject of hell. He went up and down the land preaching on hell. Mr. Munsey died in 1877 in Jonesboro, Tennessee when he was only forty-four years old. Many of his messages on the subject of hell were placed in book form.

In one of his messages entitled "Eternal Retribution," Mr. Munsey said that he was sitting in his study, musing over the Word of God, praying, and asking God to help him prepare a message. He was thinking about hell, and he began to pen some thoughts about it.

Hell may be a gloomy, desolate, and barren world whose rocks and mountains are tumbled into anarchy, but there are no blessed flowers, nodding trees, dewy vales, grassy slopes, and running streams. There are no homes, no churches, no preaching, no morality, no religion, no friendships, and no God. Then the best hell we can promise is a world of ugly ruins shrouded in night's blackest darkness where no one of the damned has a friend. It is a place filled with cursings and strifes, where are ranks and sexes herded in one promiscuous mob with the foulest demons and where every stinking cave is inhabited with fiend, gnashing ghosts, and on whose black crags ravens of despair sit and croak and where God's eternal justice plies His burning whip and remorse lays on with fiery thongs. The flashes of whips and thongs are their only light, wild without end, darkness forever. It may be some huge cavern, howling out the center of some blasted, shattered, and God-cursed planet in which the poison and the stench of ages have gathered and condensing is still on the walls, dimly lit by sulphuric torches held by grimacing and howling fiends whose sickly flickerings render the darkness in all the winding pits, chasms, and corridors but blacker. Occasional blue flames break through the fissures overhead, lick along the arches and bolts of thunder, crash through the grottos in which lost men and fallen angels may be driven from the judgment seat. The ponderous gates close and lock behind them, the key fastened to the girdle of God and the divine omnipotent installed as perpetual signal to guard the way in this darkness forever. It may be an unquenchable lake of fire and brimstone, bubbles dancing on every wave and bursting fumes and smoke threaded with serpent flames in whose ascending volumes everlasting lightning flash and cross the darkness forever.

PROVISION HAS BEEN MADE TO ESCAPE THIS PLACE OF TORMENT AND GO TO HEAVEN

The Lord Jesus summarized His ministry in Luke 19:10 when He said, *"For the Son of man is come to seek and to save that which was lost."*

This is not a discussion of good people and bad people. There are good people and bad people, and some of those good people do good deeds but are not Christian people. Some people who do bad things are people who claim to be Christian people. Let us not think about good people or bad people; let us talk about righteous people. The Bible says in Romans 3:10, *"As it is written, There is none righteous, no, not one."*

In other words, there is no one who can get to heaven on his own merit. There is only one Person who ever walked on this earth who can go straight into heaven on His own merit. That Person is Jesus Christ.

The greatest evidence that there is a real hell from which to save the souls of men is what God did in giving His only begotten Son to save us from hell. The Bible says, *"For God so loved the world, that he gave his only begotten Son, that whosoever believeth in him should not perish, but have everlasting life."*

Do not miss that word *"perish."* The Bible says, *"...should not perish, but have everlasting life."*

Why did the Lord Jesus die? Why did He go to Calvary? Why did Christ let them crown Him with thorns? Why was His face bruised and bleeding? Why was His back beaten and ripped open? Why did He have a heavy cross placed upon Him? Why did He go through the cruel mockery? Why did He pray in the Garden of Gethsemane until sweat drops of blood broke through the pores of His face? Why did He allow Himself to stand in a mockery trial and be delivered into the hands of Pilate? Why did He allow Himself to go from Pilate to Herod and then back to Pilate? Why did He allow Pilate to stand Him before a mocking crowd that cried out, "Release Barabbas and crucify Christ!" when He could have called ten thousand angels and destroyed the world? Why did He go to Calvary and let Roman soldiers drive spikes into His hands and feet and lift Him up on a cross and slam that cross into a hole prepared for it? Why did He let them strip Him of His clothing? Why did He allow people to mock Him and say jeering things to Him as He hung on the cross? Why did He cry out, *"My God, my God, why hast thou forsaken me?"* When the sun refused to shine, when the sky was like midnight at noonday, and the billows of God's wrath rolled on the Son of God and He became sin for us, He who knew no sin, why did He taste death for every man? Why did He go to Calvary and bleed and die? Because a holy, righteous, just God said, "There is a real hell and every man is a sinner and headed there."

The same God said, "But I'm not willing that any should perish so I gave my only begotten Son to take your hell for you, to bleed and die for you so you don't have to die and go to hell."

Everything we should have suffered, Jesus Christ suffered for us. Everything we should have tasted, Jesus Christ tasted. Everything we should have gone through, Jesus Christ went through. God made a way for us so that we could become righteous by having the righteousness of Jesus Christ put on our account.

The moment you ask God to forgive your sin and by faith trust the Lord Jesus as your Savior, God imputes the record of Jesus Christ on your account. He imputes His righteousness to you.

> *The greatest evidence that there is a real hell from which to save the souls of men is what God did in giving His only begotten Son to save us from hell.*

Some day when we lay down this robe of flesh, soar beyond the stars, and go to be with God, we are going to go to God's heaven and escape that awful hell because of what the Lord Jesus did for us. God made a way for us.

We point an accusing finger at people who have gone into some terrible sin, but more people in the Lord's work have wasted their lives by substituting good things for the best thing than those who have done the terrible things. We are responsible to give the gospel message to the lost.

In Romans 10:13-15 the Bible says,

> *For whosoever shall call upon the name of the Lord shall be saved. How then shall they call on him in whom they have not believed? and how shall they believe in him of whom they have not heard? and how shall they hear without a preacher? and how shall they preach, except*

they be sent? as it is written, How beautiful are the feet of them that preach the gospel of peace, and bring glad tidings of good things!

There are many families hurting and angry, greatly burdened in the bondage of Islam in the country of Saudi Arabia. There are many people, no doubt, deeply concerned about this false religion and its awful bondage. On our website, we have the gospel presentation in Arabic and English, and I pray, "Lord, show us how we can get people in that part of the world to hear the gospel. There has to be a way to penetrate the areas where people say we cannot go with the gospel."

We are responsible to give the gospel message to the lost.

There are no walls through which the gospel cannot penetrate. There is no land where God, by His Spirit, cannot get in.

What do people need? They need a clear presentation of the gospel. While I am concerned about what should be done across the world, I walk by scores of people and never give them a gospel tract or witness to them. You and I need to come to the place where the subject of hell is more than a Bible subject. It is a place.

In Arkansas something happened on a barge causing it to bump the support system for a bridge. In doing so, the bridge was destroyed. Innocent people were driving down the interstate, maybe listening to the radio or talking on a cell phone. They drove onto that bridge, and without knowing the bridge was gone, they plummeted to their death. That was a real place. It really happened.

Do you know where hell is? Hell is at the end of every Christless life. In the hospitals across our cities, on the highways, and in homes, death strikes and people are gone. Where have they gone? It is sad they are gone, but it is beyond human description to speak of the sadness and tragedy of the fact that they have gone to hell.

All of this must be settled in life by what we do with Jesus Christ. We should say, "God, help me to be a faithful witness," because the Lord Jesus has made the way to heaven.

When I was an eighteen-year-old boy, I sat in a tent crusade and listened to a man preach by the name of Dr. C.E. Autry. He preached on the word, "Lost." As I sat there and listened, Dr. Autry, in his mid-sixties, would stand up on his toes, throw his arms, raise his voice, and hold up his Bible. As I listened to him, I came to realize that he believed people were lost and going to hell.

God had been dealing with me, not about my salvation because I was a Christian, but about what I was going to do with my life. I went forward that night and knelt down in the sawdust at the altar. I said, "God, I believe You want me to give You my life to keep people out of hell."

There are no walls through which the gospel cannot penetrate. There is no land where God, by His Spirit, cannot get in.

I went back to my home. I did not go to bed. I went to the living room, got down on my knees, and I prayed. By the time I got up, it was past midnight. But I knew that God had touched my heart and He had called me to serve Him with my life.

I went to the telephone because I knew there was someone outside of my family who did not care what time of night it was;

he would be glad to hear the news. I called my pastor, Dillard Hagan. I said, "Brother Hagan, I know it's late, but I want you to know I believe God has called me to preach."

Do you know where hell is? Hell is at the end of every Christless life.

I will never forget his kind words. He said, "Clarence, I'm not surprised. I'm so happy for you. I'll do everything I can to help you."

Whether or not the Lord is calling you to preach, He is calling every Christian to try to keep people out of hell by telling them about the Lord Jesus Christ.

There is a place of torment and we can tell people how they can be saved from it. May God help us to tell them.

IS THERE A PLACE OF TORMENT?

BIBLE MEMORY VERSES

"The wicked shall be turned into hell, and all the nations that forget God."

Psalm 9:17

"So shall it be at the end of the world: the angels shall come forth, and sever the wicked from among the just, and shall cast them into the furnace of fire: there shall be wailing and gnashing of teeth."

Matthew 13:49-50

"Then shall he say also unto them on the left hand, Depart from me, ye cursed, into everlasting fire, prepared for the devil and his angels."

Matthew 25:41

"And these shall go away into everlasting punishment: but the righteous into life eternal."

Matthew 25:46

"There was a certain rich man, which was clothed in purple and fine linen, and fared sumptuously every day: and there was a certain beggar named Lazarus, which was laid at his gate, full of sores, and desiring to be fed with the crumbs which fell from the rich man's table: moreover the dogs came and licked his sores. And it came to pass, that the beggar died, and was carried by the angels into Abraham's bosom: the rich man also died, and was buried; and in hell he lift up his eyes, being in torments, and seeth Abraham afar off, and Lazarus in his bosom."

Luke 16:19-23

"And to you who are troubled rest with us, when the Lord Jesus shall be revealed from heaven with his mighty angels, in flaming fire taking vengeance on them that know not God, and that obey not the gospel of our Lord Jesus Christ: who shall be punished with everlasting destruction from the presence of the Lord, and from the glory of his power."

II Thessalonians 1:7-9

"And of some have compassion, making a difference: and others save with fear, pulling them out of the fire; hating even the garment spotted by the flesh."

Jude 22-23

"And the beast was taken, and with him the false prophet that wrought miracles before him, with which he deceived them that had received the mark of the beast, and them that worshipped his image. These both were cast alive into a lake of fire burning with brimstone."

Revelation 19:20

"And whosoever was not found written in the book of life was cast into the lake of fire."

Revelation 20:15

Chapter Four

ARE WE PERSONALLY ACCOUNTABLE TO GOD?

ur local church is a group of baptized believers who have trusted Christ as Savior and have voluntarily joined themselves together to carry out the Great Commission. We identify ourselves as Baptist people, and we have certain distinctives of our faith.

The Bible, the Word of God, is the sole authority for our faith and practice. If the Bible speaks about something, then we should speak about it. If the Bible is silent on a subject, then we are to be silent on that subject. We are people of the Book. We make no apology for this. All that we believe and teach we find in the Word of God.

When we say that the Bible is the sole authority, we are speaking of all the Scriptures, the whole and its parts. We should preach the whole counsel of God. In the Bible we find the gospel–the death, burial, and resurrection of Jesus Christ. We should proclaim the gospel because Jesus Christ said that we are to take the gospel message to every creature. When we open the sixty-six books of the Bible, we find more than the gospel. Of course, that scarlet thread of redemption runs through all the Bible, but the whole counsel of God must be proclaimed.

> *It is impossible to be a spiritual person without being a Scriptural person. We need to know and live the Word of God.*

If we are going to be spiritual people, we must be Scriptural people. It is impossible to be a spiritual person without being a scriptural person. We need to know and live the Word of God.

The Bible says in Romans 14:11-12, *"For it is written, As I live, saith the Lord, every knee shall bow to me, and every tongue shall confess to God. So then every one of us shall give account of himself to God."*

Let us consider the twelfth verse, *"Every one of us shall give account of himself to God,"* or the subject of soul liberty, our personal accountability to God.

In our nation we hear people talk about religious tolerance. Religious tolerance is something created by government. It is a "gift" from government. Religious tolerance is something man has made. Soul liberty is something God established when He created us. We find a clear teaching of this in His Word. Soul liberty is a gift from God! God's Word says in Galatians 5:1, *"Stand fast therefore in the liberty wherewith Christ hath made us free, and be not entangled again with the yoke of bondage."*

Soul liberty does not rest upon the legal documents of our nation–it is rooted in the Word of God. This individual freedom of the soul is inherent in man's nature as God created him. Man is responsible for his choices, but he is free to choose.

This powerful declaration about our Baptist position was made by J.D. Freeman in 1905:

> Our demand has been not simply for religious toleration, but religious liberty; not sufferance merely, but freedom; and that not for ourselves alone, but for all men. We did not stumble upon the doctrine. It inheres in the very essence of our belief. Christ is Lord of all....The conscience is the servant only of God, and is not subject to the will of man. This truth has indestructible life. Crucify it and the third day it will rise again. Bury it in the sepulcher and the stone will be rolled away, while the keepers become as dead men....Steadfastly refusing to bend our necks under the yoke of bondage, we have scrupulously withheld our hands from imposing that yoke upon others....Of martyr blood our hands are clean. We have never invoked the sword of temporal power to aid the sword of the Spirit. We have never passed an ordinance inflicting a civic disability on any man because of his religious views, be he Protestant or Papist, Jew, or Turk, or infidel. In this regard there is no blot on our escutcheon.

> *Soul liberty is a gift from God!*

Remember that, when we are talking about individual soul liberty and the relationship of the church and the state, in America the Constitution does not place the church over the state or the state over the church. Most importantly, Scripture places them side by side, each operating independently of the other. This means there is freedom in the church and freedom in the state. Each is sovereign within the sphere of the authority God has given to each of them (Matthew 22:21).

Read carefully this statement made by Charles Spurgeon concerning Baptist people:

> We believe that the Baptists are the original Christians. We did not commence our existence at the Reformation, we were reformers before Luther or Calvin were born; we never came from the Church of Rome, for we were never in it, but we have an unbroken line up to the apostles themselves. We have always existed from the very days of Christ, and our principles, sometimes veiled and forgotten, like a river which may travel underground for a little season, have always had honest and holy adherents. Persecuted alike by Romanists and Protestants of almost every sect, yet there has never existed a government holding Baptist principles which persecuted others; nor, I believe, any body of Baptists ever held it to be right to put the consciences of others under the control of man. We have ever been ready to suffer, as our martyrologies will prove, but we are not ready to accept any help from the State, to prostitute the purity of the Bride of Christ to any alliance with Government, and we will never make the Church, although the Queen, the despot over the consciences of men.

This a marvelous statement about Baptist people. I am rather troubled when I see so many people who claim to be Baptists who do not understand why they are Baptists. We should be able to defend our position and do it biblically. If we are people who know and love the Lord and His Word and if the Bible is our sole authority for faith and practice, then we have no reason to be ashamed of the position we take. May God not only help us to take this position, but to take it with holy boldness and compassion. May He help us to be able to take His Word in hand and heart and defend what we believe to a lost and dying world.

So much of what we have to enjoy in our country can be credited to Baptist people. For example, if you study the history of our nation, you are going to find that the Virginia Baptists were almost solely responsible for the First Amendment being added to our Constitution. We enjoy this freedom of separation of church and state, and the freedom to worship God as our conscience dictates because of the influence of Baptist people on the Founding Fathers of our nation.

We have a country that has been so influenced that we do not believe it is right to exercise any control or coercion of any kind over the souls of men. Where did this conviction come from? We find it in the Bible, but someone imparted it to the Founding Fathers. It became the law of the land, and it should remain the law of the land. We need to understand it. It comes out of the clear teaching of God's Word concerning the subject of soul liberty.

My wife and I have had the privilege of visiting the land of England a number of times. England is a marvelous place to visit. There are places where people were martyred for their faith, giving their lives for what they believed. The religious persecution came as a result of the laws of the land. Although many Baptists have been martyred, you will never find Baptist people persecuting anyone anywhere for his faith, no matter what his faith may be.

Let us take some serious subjects from God's Word and attempt to give clear distinctives we have as Baptists, especially emphasizing the matter of soul liberty. The word *Baptist* can be remembered by an acrostic which is often used to represent our distinctives.

B is for *biblical authority*. The Bible is the sole authority for our faith and practice.

A stands for the *autonomy* of the local church. Every church we find in the New Testament was a self-governing church with only Christ as the head.

P represents the *priesthood* of believers and the access we have to God through Jesus Christ.

T stands for the *two church officers*–pastors and deacons. We find these officers in the New Testament.

I stands for *individual soul liberty.* Most people, when asked, say that the sole authority of the Scripture in our faith and practice is the single, most important distinctive of our faith. However, if we did not have individual soul liberty, we could not come to the convictions we have on all other matters.

S stands for a *saved church membership.*

T represents *two church ordinances*–baptism and the Lord's Supper. These are the things that Jesus Christ ordered that we do. Both of these ordinances are pictures of His sacrifice for us on the cross of Calvary.

S stands for *separation of church and state.* Of course, this has been reinterpreted in our times to be something entirely different from what our Founding Fathers meant for it to be. The ACLU and People for the American Way define separation of church and state as an obligation of the state to erase every vestige of Christianity from our public institutions. This was certainly not the intent of our Founding Fathers.

These are the distinctives of Baptist people. Baptist distinctives are often given in this acrostic form so they are easier to remember.

PERSONAL ACCOUNTABILITY TO GOD

We find this accountability in the opening verses of God's Word. When God created man, He created man capable of giving a personal account of himself to God. God did not create puppets; He created people. He gave man the right to choose. That is why we find the man Adam choosing to sin and to disobey God in Genesis chapter three. Of his own volition he chose to sin and disobey God. Genesis 1:27 says, *"So God created man in his own image, in the image of God created he him; male and female created he them."* We were made in God's image, and when God made us in His image, He made us with the ability to choose. Eve was deceived, but Adam chose to die rather than to live without Eve. He willingly chose to disobey the Lord.

It is not right to try to force one's religion or belief upon another individual. He has a God-given right to believe anything he wishes to believe. This does not mean, however, that he can be a Christian by believing anything he wishes to believe, because Jesus Christ said that there is only one way to heaven. He said in John 14:6, *"I am the way, the truth, and the life: no man cometh unto the Father, but by me."* He is the only way to God. The only way of salvation is the Lord Jesus Christ.

In this age of tolerance, people say that nothing is really wrong. The same people who say that no way of believing is wrong will not accept the truth that one belief can be the only way that is right. The truth is, you may believe anything you choose, but God has declared that there is only one way to Him and that is through His Son, Jesus Christ. He is the only way of salvation–that is why He suffered and died for our sins. The only way to know God is through His Son, the Lord Jesus Christ.

> *The only way to know God is through His Son, the Lord Jesus Christ.*

Someone is certain to ask, "Who are you to declare that everyone else's religion is wrong?" We are saying that everyone has a right to choose his own way, but God has clearly taught us in His Word that there is only one way to Him. The Lord Jesus says in John 10:9, *"I am the door: by me if any man enter in, he shall be saved, and shall go in and out, and find pasture."*

No human being is going to live on this earth without being sinned against by others. Many children are sinned against greatly by their own parents. However, we cannot go through life blaming others for the person we are, because God has made us in such a way that we have an individual accountability to God. This comes out of our soul liberty and our right to choose and respond to things in a way that God would have us respond to them. God has made us in His image. Again, He did not make us puppets or robots; He made us people, created in His image with the ability to choose our own way.

Romans 14:11-12 says, *"For it is written, As I live, saith the Lord, every knee shall bow to me, and every tongue shall confess to God. So then every one of us shall give account of himself to God."* We are responsible because we have direct access to God. God has given us the Word of God, the Holy Spirit, and access to the Throne by prayer. We, therefore, must answer personally to God at the judgment seat because God communicates to us directly.

We are living at a time when people do not like to be held personally accountable for their actions. The truth of the Word of God is that every individual is personally accountable to God. You are personally accountable to God. In other words, you are going to meet God in judgment some day. I am going to meet God in judgment some day. All of us are going to stand before the Lord some day and answer to Him. We are individually accountable to God. One of our Crown College professors, Dr. Robert Dalton, states, "Since the state cannot answer for us to God, it has no right to dictate our conscience."

We live in a country where there are many false religions. As Baptist people, we would defend the right of anyone in our land to worship as he sees fit to worship. This is unheard of in most of the world. If a man is a Moslem, I do not agree with his Islamic religion, but I must defend his right to worship as he sees fit to worship. The clear teaching of the Catholic church teaches that salvation comes through Mary, but this is not the teaching of the Bible. We must take a stand against false religions, but we must also defend the right of people to worship as they choose to worship. Why? Because individual soul liberty is a gift from God to every human being.

The truth of the Word of God is that every individual is personally accountable to God. You are personally accountable to God.

If we truly believe that the Bible teaches individual soul liberty and personal accountability to God, then it is a truth that will endure to all generations.

John Bunyan is the man who gave us *Pilgrim's Progress*. This wonderful book was planned during Bunyan's prison experience and written when he was released. The trial of John Bunyan took place on October 3, 1660. John Bunyan spent twelve years in jail for his convictions about individual soul liberty, failure to attend the Church of England, and for preaching the Word of God.

During his trial, John stood before Judge Wingate who was interested in hearing John Bunyan state his case. Judge Wingate said, "In that case, then, this court would be profoundly interested in your response to them."

> *If we truly believe that the Bible teaches individual soul liberty and personal accountability to God, then it is a truth that will endure to all generations.*

Part of John Bunyan's response follows:

Thank you, M'lord. And may I say that I am grateful for the opportunity to respond. Firstly, the depositions speak the truth. I have never attended services in the Church of England, nor do I intend ever to do so. Secondly, it is no secret that I preach the Word of God whenever, wherever, and to whomever He pleases to grant me opportunity to do so.

Having said that, M'lord, there is a weightier issue that I am constrained to address. I have no choice but to acknowledge my awareness of the law which I am accused of transgressing. Likewise, I have no choice but to confess my guilt in my transgression of it. As true as these things are, I must affirm that I neither regret

breaking the law, nor repent of having broken it.
Further, I must warn you that I have no intention
in future of conforming to it. It is, on its face, an
unjust law, a law against which honorable men
cannot shrink from protesting. In truth, M'lord,
it violates an infinitely higher law–the right of
every man to seek God in his own way,
unhindered by any temporal power. That,
M'lord, is my response.

Remember that Bunyan was responding as to why he would
not do all that he was doing for God within the confines of the
Church of England. The transcription goes on to say:

Judge Wingate: This court would remind you,
sir, that we are not here to debate the merits of
the law. We are here to determine if you are, in
fact, guilty of violating it.

John Bunyan: Perhaps, M'lord, that is why
you are here, but it is most certainly not why I
am here. I am here because you compel me to be
here. All I ask is to be left alone to preach and to
teach as God directs me. As, however, I must be
here, I cannot fail to use these circumstances to
speak against what I know to be an unjust and
odious edict.

Judge Wingate: Let me understand you. You
are arguing that every man has a right, given him
by Almighty God, to seek the Deity in his own
way, even if he chooses without the benefit of
the English Church?

Bunyan: That is precisely what I am arguing,
M'lord. Or without benefit of any church.

Judge Wingate: Do you know what you are saying? What of Papist and Quakers? What of pagan Mohammedans? Have these the right to seek God in their own misguided way?

Bunyan: Even these, M'lord.

Judge Wingate: May I ask if you are particularly sympathetic to the views of these or other such deviant religious societies?

Bunyan: I am not, M'lord.

Judge Wingate: Yet, you affirm a God-given right to hold any alien religious doctrine that appeals to the warped minds of men?

Bunyan: I do, M'lord.

Judge Wingate: I find your views impossible of belief. And what of those who, if left to their own devices, would have no interest in things heavenly? Have they the right to be allowed to continue unmolested in their error?

Bunyan: It is my fervent belief that they do, M'lord.

Judge Wingate: And on what basis, might I ask, can you make such rash affirmations?

Bunyan: On the basis, M'lord, that a man's religious views—or lack of them—are matters between his conscience and his God, and are not the business of the Crown, the Parliament, or even, with all due respect, M'lord, of this court. However much I may be in disagreement with another man's sincerely held religious beliefs, neither I nor any other may disallow his right to hold those beliefs. No man's rights in these affairs are secure if every other man's rights are not equally secure.

I do not know of anyone who could have expressed the whole idea of soul liberty in the words of man any more clearly than Bunyan stated in 1660. Every man can seek God as he pleases. This means that we cannot force our religious faith or teaching on anyone. It means clearly that no one can be coerced into being a Baptist and believing what we believe. It means that we can do no arm-twisting, or anything of that sort, to make anyone believe what we believe. Every man has been created by God with the ability to choose to follow God or to follow some other god.

Personal accountability to God is a distinctive of our faith. It is something we believe, and out of this distinctive come other distinctives that we identify with as Baptist people.

THE PRIESTHOOD OF EVERY BELIEVER

The priesthood of the believer means that every believer can go to God through the merit of Jesus Christ. Christ and Christ alone is the only way to God. All of us who have trusted Christ as Savior enjoy the glorious privilege of the priesthood of the believer and can access God through the merits of our Lord and Savior Jesus Christ.

The Bible says in I Timothy 2:1-6,

> *I exhort therefore, that, first of all, supplications, prayers, intercessions, and giving of thanks, be made for all men; for kings, and for all that are in authority; that we may lead a quiet and peaceable life in all godliness and honesty.*

For this is good and acceptable in the sight of God our Saviour; who will have all men to be saved, and to come unto the knowledge of the truth. For there is one God, and one mediator between God and men, the man Christ Jesus; who gave himself a ransom for all, to be testified in due time.

> Personal accountability to God is a distinctive of our faith.

Take special note of verse five, *"For there is one God, and one mediator between God and men, the man Christ Jesus."* Any man, anywhere in this world can go to God through the Lord Jesus Christ.

I Peter 2:9 says, *"But ye are a chosen generation, a royal priesthood, an holy nation, a peculiar people; that ye should shew forth the praises of him who hath called you out of darkness into his marvellous light."*

You have access to God. You can personally talk to God. You can take your needs to the Lord. Whatever your needs are, you can take those needs to the Lord. You, as an individual Christian, can go to God through the Lord Jesus Christ, your High Priest who *"ever liveth to make intercession"* for you (Hebrews 7:25).

We have no merit of our own. We do not accumulate merit. People may make reference to a time of meritorious service someone has rendered, but we cannot build up "good works" that get us through to God. Each day, we must come before God as needy sinners approaching Him through the finished work of Christ and Christ alone.

The Bible teaches the personal accountability of every human being to God. We cannot force our religion on anyone or make anyone a believer. We cannot force someone to be a Christian. Think of how wrong it is to take babies and allow them later in life to think they have become Christians by an act of infant baptism. Yes, they have a right to practice infant baptism, but we do not believe this is biblical because faith cannot be forced or coerced.

If I have discovered the truth in Christ and believe that God's Word is inerrant, infallible, and eternal, certainly I want my own children to believe that. I have no greater joy than that they walk in truth, but I cannot make my sons Christians. They must choose Christ of their own will.

I have six beautiful grandchildren. There is a real heaven and a real hell. The Bible clearly teaches this. The only way to heaven and the only way to miss hell is by trusting Christ and Christ alone as Savior. However, I cannot make those grandchildren Christians no matter how much I desire to. They must individually trust Christ as their Savior.

There are places in the world where the state is under a religion. There are places in the world where religion is under the state–the state controls the fate of people. This is not taught in the Bible. Then, there are countries like ours where the church and the state operate side by side.

THE POWER OF INFLUENCE

Where does this teaching of the priesthood of every believer and our personal accountability to God lead us? It leads us to realize the importance of the power of influence. This is the tool God has given us. I want to give you an Old Testament example of the New Testament church. There is a difference between Israel and the church; I am not trying to place the church in the Old Testament, but let us use this as an illustration.

Judges 21:25 tells us, *"In those days there was no king in Israel: every man did that which was right in his own eyes."* Can you imagine that? This was a land of anarchy. Every man did what was right in his own eyes. In the days of the judges, every man wanted to do what he thought was right with no fixed point of reference.

The more churches get like the world, the less influence they are going to have in the world.

God's Word continues to describe this time of judges in Ruth 1:1, *"Now it came to pass in the days when the judges ruled, that there was a famine in the land."* God begins to tell us about a man named Elimelech, his wife Naomi, and his sons. He brings us to the beautiful love story of Ruth and Boaz. God tells us that at the same time in which the judges ruled, when there was anarchy in the land, this beautiful love story of Boaz and Ruth took place.

This story gives us interesting insight on the responsibility of the Christian and the church. In the midst of everything that is going on, we are to share the beautiful love story of the Lord Jesus Christ and His bride. We need to tell people about the Savior.

The same truth is found throughout the Word of God. Philippians 2:15 states, *"That ye may be blameless and harmless, the sons of God, without rebuke, in the midst of a crooked and perverse nation, among whom ye shine as lights in the world."*

We are *"in the midst of a crooked and perverse nation."* This is why the Lord Jesus said in Matthew 5:16, *"Let your light so shine before men, that they may see your good works, and glorify your Father which is in heaven."* Let your light shine!

The more churches get like the world, the less influence they are going to have in the world. Preaching ceases, and churches only have dialogue. Singing that is sacred is taken out, and the world's music comes in. What so many are attempting to do in order to build up their ministry is actually what will cause the demise of their ministry. We will never make a difference without being willing to be different. It is Christ who makes us different.

We cannot force people to become Christians or force our religion on people. It is not right to violate another man's will; he must choose of his own volition to trust Christ or reject Christ. When we understand this, then we understand the powerful tool of influence. We must live godly lives and be what God wants us to be. We must be lights in a dark world as we live in the midst of a crooked generation. The only tool we have to use is influence, not force. As we separate ourselves to God and live godly lives, only then do we have a testimony.

> *Separation to God and from the world is not the enemy of evangelism; it is the essential of evangelism.*

Separation *to* God and *from* the world is not the enemy of evangelism; it is the essential of evangelism. There can be no evangelism without separation to God from the world because we have no other tool to use. We cannot make people believe what we believe to be the truth. They must choose of their own will. We must so identify with the Lord Jesus in His beauty, glory, and holiness that He will be lifted up, and people will come to Him.

As this world becomes increasingly worse, the more off-the-wall and ridiculous we will appear to an unbelieving world. The temptation will come again and again for us to simply cave in.

It is because of what we find in the Bible about soul liberty, personal accountability, and the priesthood of every believer that we must use the power of influence to win the lost to Christ. If we conform to the world, we lose our influence.

May the Lord help us to be unashamed to bear His reproach and be identified with our Lord Jesus Christ.

ARE WE PERSONALLY ACCOUNTABLE TO GOD?

BIBLE MEMORY VERSES

"For it is written, As I live, saith the Lord, every knee shall bow to me, and every tongue shall confess to God. So then every one of us shall give account of himself to God."

Romans 14:11-12

"Stand fast therefore in the liberty wherewith Christ hath made us free, and be not entangled again with the yoke of bondage."

Galatians 5:1

"In whom we have boldness and access with confidence by the faith of him."

Ephesians 3:12

"That ye may be blameless and harmless, the sons of God, without rebuke, in the midst of a crooked and perverse nation, among whom ye shine as lights in the world."

Philippians 2:15

"For there is one God, and one mediator between God and men, the man Christ Jesus; who gave himself a ransom for all, to be testified in due time."

I Timothy 2:5-6

"Let us therefore come boldly unto the throne of grace, that we may obtain mercy, and find grace to help in time of need."

Hebrews 4:16

"Having therefore, brethren, boldness to enter into the holiest by the blood of Jesus, by a new and living way, which he hath consecrated for us, through the veil, that is to say, his flesh; and having an high priest over the house of God; let us draw near with a true heart in full assurance of faith, having our hearts sprinkled from an evil conscience, and our bodies washed with pure water."

Hebrews 10:19-22

"But ye are a chosen generation, a royal priesthood, an holy nation, a peculiar people; that ye should shew forth the praises of him who hath called you out of darkness into his marvellous light."

I Peter 2:9

Chapter Five

DOES CHARACTER COUNT?

 here is one word in Proverbs 19:1 that should catch the attention of all of us who want to please the Lord. The Bible says, *"Better is the poor that walketh in his integrity, than he that is perverse in his lips, and is a fool."* Place special emphasis on the powerful word in the heart of this verse, *"integrity."*

Integrity is something that should characterize every one of God's children. When we speak of someone's character, we are speaking about what he is in the heart. When we speak of someone's reputation, we are speaking of what others think of him. People may affect our reputation by what they say or do not say or how they respond when our name is called. People may have some bearing upon our reputation, but all of us determine our character by how we respond personally to the Lord Jesus Christ.

Character is what we are; reputation is what others think we are. When Abraham Lincoln was President, he said, "Character is the tree; reputation is the shadow." The shadow is determined by the tree. If we guard our character, we can trust God to guard our reputation. Our character, what we are, the makeup of our lives, should be characterized by integrity. No amount of ability or personality can serve as a fitting substitute for integrity.

> *Our crisis is not simply a crisis of conduct; it is a crisis of character.*

The word *"integrity"* is a powerful word meaning "to be complete; together in honesty; nothing to hide or fear; transparent; together." It is the work of God to put things together. It is the work of the Devil to tear things apart, to separate, to divide. A person with integrity is not divided. People with integrity have nothing to hide.

So many of us are not whole. What we lack is integrity. No one can take integrity from us. If we lose integrity, it is because we give it up of our own volition.

A national news magazine recently remarked that America has become a nation of liars. No one, from politicians to preachers, can be trusted. With all that is happening, they had good reason to make that statement. We need a revival of integrity. It should begin in the church among God's people. Our crisis is not simply a crisis of conduct; it is a crisis of character.

There is a difference between what is biblical, what is considered to be moral, and what is legal. In a society, laws are passed to show what things are legal and what things are illegal. Also in a society, people determine what is moral and what is immoral. The mores, or moral standards, of a society are always shifting and changing. What was considered to be immoral twenty years ago may be considered moral in this day. There are things that are legal that we do not consider to be moral, and there are things that the world considers to be moral that are still not biblical.

As children of God, we are called to live on a standard that is higher than what the world calls moral and higher than what the world may say is legal. We are to live on a biblical standard and not be patterned after the world. The rest of the world may lie and cheat their way through life and think it is acceptable to do so, but God's children must hold to a biblical standard and live a life of integrity.

The cause of Christ suffers reproach from a lack of character. There are many people laughing at leaders who should be respected. We have traded holy living for the pursuit of happiness. We are sadly lacking when it comes to integrity. Determine to be a person of integrity. In your heart, be truthful, honest, and right with God. Be whole.

No one can take integrity from us. If we lose integrity, it is because we give it up of our own volition.

As our Lord gave what we call the "Sermon on the Mount," He said to His disciples in Matthew 5:13-14, *"Ye are the salt of the earth: but if the salt have lost his savour, wherewith shall it be salted? it is thenceforth good for nothing, but to be cast out, and to be trodden under foot of men. Ye are the light of the world. A city that is set on an hill cannot be hid."*

Christ said we are salt. The chemical makeup of salt is not destroyed when it is mixed with other ingredients, but the power of the salt is lost. One can still find the elements that make the salt, but it loses its strength and power when it becomes polluted with other ingredients. Our Lord said that we are the salt of the earth, the preserving influence of righteousness and holy living, people of integrity.

> *The most respected people in the community should be those who name the name of Jesus Christ.*

Christians should be believable. The most respected people in the community should be those who name the name of Jesus Christ. Whether you are a pastor, a deacon, a Sunday School teacher, or a member of a Bible-believing, Bible-preaching church, to be identified with God's work should mean that you have integrity.

We have a testimony to guard. Our Lord's name must not be put to shame because we have lost integrity. We have a testimony to protect—the high, holy name of our Lord. It cannot be protected unless we are people of integrity.

In the Bible, the Lord gives testimony concerning Job. The Bible says in Job 2:1-3,

> *Again there was a day when the sons of God came to present themselves before the LORD, and Satan came also among them to present himself before the LORD. And the LORD said unto Satan, From whence comest thou? And Satan answered the LORD, and said, From going to and fro in the earth, and from walking up and down in it. And the LORD said unto Satan, Hast thou considered my servant Job, that there is none like him in the earth, a perfect and an upright man, one that feareth God, and escheweth evil? and still he*

*holdeth fast his integrity, although thou movedst
me against him, to destroy him without cause.*

The testimony of God concerning Job is that he was a man of integrity. Remember what God says in Proverbs 19:1, *"Better is the poor that walketh in his integrity, than he that is perverse in his lips, and is a fool."* The word *"better"* here means this is a matter of choice. Some people are people of integrity, and some are not. Those who make the right choice are those who choose to walk in integrity. I wish I could say that every Christian is a person of integrity.

You may say, "Honesty is the best policy." Honesty is not the *best* policy—for a man of integrity, it is the *only* policy. This policy is not only for people in the ministry; it is for every child of God. With all the idolatrous things done in the name of the Lord and all the scandalous things reported in the media about preachers, no wonder the cause of Christ is suffering reproach. We need a revival of integrity.

> *Honesty is not the best policy— for a man of integrity, it is the only policy.*

The Bible says in Proverbs 11:3, *"The integrity of the upright shall guide them..."* How do I do what is right each day? The Bible answers, *"The integrity of the upright shall guide them: but the perverseness of transgressors shall destroy them."* The "situation ethics" crowd has no fixed point of reference and believes in telling anything anytime if it works for their good. They say, "Whether true or false, go ahead and tell it." Trying to escape unwanted outcome by telling anything they choose to tell, whether it be true or false, is not the life of integrity. The Bible says that this crowd is going to end in destruction. Their perverse ways are going to come back like a boomerang and destroy them. Have we forgotten that everything we sow we also reap? We reap what we sow, and we reap more than we sow.

I wish that every person I speak to on the telephone were an honest person. I wish everyone I dealt with in the ministry had integrity. Think how much easier our lives would be, how much pain we could avoid, if we were people of integrity.

> *Think how much easier our lives would be, how much pain we could avoid, if we were people of integrity.*

If you are married, you want to believe that your spouse is a person of integrity, that even when you are not present, your mate will do right because it is right to do right. You want to be married to a person of integrity, a person you can put your confidence and trust in, knowing that no matter where he may be, he will do what is right. You want to rear children who have integrity so you can trust them. When trust is gone, it is so difficult to build it back. Little do we know and seem to understand how devastating it is to be unable to trust people. A person of integrity is someone who can be trusted.

I am not on a crusade to try to promote integrity at the grocery store or integrity at the factory; I am on a crusade to see a restoration of integrity in the work of God. May every member of our churches be known as a person of integrity.

God says that it is better to have integrity than to lie your way through life. Being a person of integrity is its own reward. You can sleep better at night if you have integrity. Your conscience will not constantly smite you if you have integrity. Integrity will guide you.

When Job was nearing the end of his testings in Job chapter twenty-seven, notice what he said in verses one through five,

> *Moreover Job continued his parable, and said, As God liveth, who hath taken away my judgment; and the Almighty, who hath vexed my soul; all the while my breath is in me, and the spirit of God is in my nostrils; my lips shall not speak wickedness, nor my tongue utter deceit. God forbid that I should justify you: till I die I will not remove mine integrity from me.*

Job said, "As long as I live, I will be a man of integrity." What a powerful statement! The Word of God says in Job 31:1-6,

> *I made a covenant with mine eyes; why then should I think upon a maid? For what portion of God is there from above? and what inheritance of the Almighty from on high? Is not destruction to the wicked? and a strange punishment to the workers of iniquity? Doth not he see my ways, and count all my steps? If I have walked with vanity, or if my foot hath hasted to deceit; let me be weighed in an even balance, that God may know mine integrity.*

He said, "God sees everything I do. I cannot fool Him. God knows every step I take. God knows the thoughts of my mind. May God put me on the scale and see that I am a man of integrity."

It is painful to think that people around the world are saying that America has become a nation of liars. Greed has driven us to break all limits of honesty and decency. We have lied in order to get ahead. I hate to think about the reputation of my nation in the eyes of the world, being a nation without integrity. More than that, it grieves me to think that in many places the church is not trusted. Let us pay our bills on time. Let us give our word and keep it. Let us preach the truth, stand boldly in this cowardly age, and be people of integrity.

Does the Lord reveal anywhere in His Word how we can get integrity? The Lord gives us the keys to integrity in the book of Job.

> *Greed has driven us to break all limits of honesty and decency. We have lied in order to get ahead.*

There is a battle going on. The Devil does not really want me or you. He wants to bring reproach upon the name of the Lord. I am only a means to his end if he can get me. Though ministers and ministries have been discredited in our day, the shame has been poured upon the name of Jesus Christ. This should trouble us greatly.

We are not ready for this fight we are in. The fight is a daily battle with the Devil and his forces. The preparation is personal preparation. In this crisis hour of human history, a person is a hypocrite who says he loves the Lord and does not attend church faithfully. Those who attend Bible-believing churches are allowing God an opportunity to speak to their hearts through His Word, but our preparation must go beyond our church services. It must extend to our private lives where we prepare personally to wage war with the Devil.

INTEGRITY COMES FROM KNOWING GOD

The Devil said, "I'm going to get Job." God said, "He is a man of integrity." As the Lord spoke of Job, He revealed the key to integrity when He asked Satan in Job 2:3, *"Hast thou considered my servant Job?"* When speaking of Job, the Lord used the personal possessive pronoun, *"my."* Integrity comes from knowing God. It does not come from knowing *about* Him, but knowing Him. We can fake it, but there is no substitute for knowing Him. We should know the Lord in salvation. Know that you are saved. Know without doubt, with peace and assurance, that you have given your heart and life to Jesus Christ, that you belong to Him, that you are His child.

Integrity comes from knowing God. Know Him as you commune with Him daily. In Philippians 3:10, the apostle Paul, after twenty years or more in the ministry, wrote the church in Philippi saying, *"That I may know him."*

God said of Job, "He is My servant. He lives for Me. He belongs to Me. He knows Me." I want God to say of me, "That man knows Me." There is no integrity for life, no wholeness, no completeness unless we first know the Lord. He makes us whole.

INTEGRITY COMES FROM FEARING GOD

The Lord asked Satan in Job 2:3, *"Hast thou considered my servant Job, that there is none like him in the earth, a perfect and an upright man, one that feareth God...?"* Integrity comes from fearing God.

Why should a person do what is right? Because he fears God. A fellow may say, "I'm not going to live in sin because I'm afraid I'll get AIDS." That man should do right because he fears God and because God tells him to live righteously. Someone may say, "I'm going to tell the truth because I'm afraid I will get caught in a lie." No, he should tell the truth because he fears God and he knows that God keeps an account of every word we speak and every thought we have. This will create integrity. You may say, "I'm afraid my parents will catch me, so I'm going to stay out of trouble." It is great to obey your parents, but you should do right because you fear God.

God said to the Devil, "Job fears Me." We try to weaken this idea of fearing God into less than it is. We talk about fear being reverential respect until we have God pacified like some bearded old man who is not able to cope with the problems of our day. We respect Him like we would one of our elders. How ridiculous! We are talking about the God of heaven and earth, who created the world and made us from dust. We are talking about our Creator, not some weak being who is unable to deal with the crisis in our world. Our God still sits on the throne of the universe and has everything under His control. Integrity comes from fearing God. Do you fear Him?

> *All of us need to realize that we are ultimately, personally accountable to God.*

For years I would say to my children, "Boys, you are supposed to do right." I spent much time telling them how to sit, how to eat, how to shake hands, how to greet people, how to interview for a job, how to dress properly, and everything I could think of about life. They knew what they were supposed to do when their daddy came around, but I think the greatest thing God ever led me to do with my children is to help them understand that beyond being accountable to me, they are each personally accountable to God.

We are all personally accountable to God. When we get to the end of life on earth, we are not going to stand before our earthly fathers. We will stand before God. Thank God for every authority figure who can help us. Thank God for pastors, teachers, Sunday School workers, deacons, and everyone in any position of leadership, but all of us need to realize that we are ultimately, personally accountable to God.

All the talk about terrible things that can happen to people in our day should not be our motivation. Let us fear God, not disease. Let us fear God, not people. God said, "My servant Job fears Me." Know God and fear God.

INTEGRITY COMES FROM LIVING FOR GOD

The Bible says in Job 2:3, *"...and escheweth evil?"* The word *"escheweth"* means to remove one's foot from the path of evil.

Every day we must make decisions. God said, "My servant hears Me and escheweth evil. He removes his foot from what is wrong." The first step on a path in the wrong direction may look tremendously inviting, but think of where it leads. Biblical separation is separation *unto* the Lord and *from* the world. This is holy living–living not to be seen of men but living for God.

I am with my wife every opportunity I have to be with her. Someone may say, "You are married to her. You are supposed to be with her." This is true, but there is a higher motive. It is not just because I am supposed to be with her; it is because I love being with her. This is the greater motive. One may say, "A Christian is supposed to stop doing wrong and start doing right." That is right, but if one knows and fears God, he will do right, not because he is supposed to, but because he loves God and wants to please the Lord.

> *Biblical separation is separation unto the Lord and from the world.*

When God referred to Job, He said in Job 2:3, *"Hast thou considered my servant Job, that there is none like him in the earth, a perfect and an upright man, one that feareth God, and escheweth evil? and still he holdeth fast his integrity."* If you desire to be a person of integrity, you must know the Lord, fear Him, and live for Him. This will produce integrity.

Integrity cannot be taken from us. It must be voluntarily surrendered and given up. As a nation we are laughing our way to hell in a parade of people without integrity. In this day of integrity crisis, remember that character counts!

DOES CHARACTER COUNT?

BIBLE MEMORY VERSES

"And the LORD said unto Satan, Hast thou considered my servant Job, that there is none like him in the earth, a perfect and an upright man, one that feareth God, and escheweth evil? and still he holdeth fast his integrity, although thou movedst me against him, to destroy him without cause."

Job 2:3

"God forbid that I should justify you: till I die I will not remove mine integrity from me."

Job 27:5

"I made a covenant with mine eyes; why then should I think upon a maid? For what portion of God is there from above? and what inheritance of the Almighty from on high? Is not destruction to the wicked? and a strange punishment to the workers of iniquity? Doth not he see my ways, and count all my steps? If I have walked with vanity, or if my foot hath hasted to deceit; let me be weighed in an even balance, that God may know mine integrity."

Job 31:1-6

"The LORD shall judge the people: judge me, O LORD, according to my righteousness, and according to mine integrity that is in me."

Psalm 7:8

"Let integrity and uprightness preserve me; for I wait on thee."
Psalm 25:21

"Judge me, O LORD; for I have walked in mine integrity: I have trusted also in the LORD; therefore I shall not slide."
Psalm 26:1

"But as for me, I will walk in mine integrity: redeem me, and be merciful unto me."

Psalm 26:11

"And as for me, thou upholdest me in mine integrity, and settest me before thy face for ever."

Psalm 41:12

"The integrity of the upright shall guide them: but the perverseness of transgressors shall destroy them."

Proverbs 11:3

"Better is the poor that walketh in his integrity, than he that is perverse in his lips, and is a fool."

Proverbs 19:1

"The just man walketh in his integrity: his children are blessed after him."

Proverbs 20:7

Chapter Six

WHAT DOES THE LORD SAY ABOUT LIQUOR?

n the book of Habakkuk, the Lord spoke to the prophet Habakkuk about His judgment upon the nation of Babylon. Babylon was going to come down upon Judah, destroy the land, and carry the people captive. Habakkuk cried out to God and said, "Lord, but they are so wicked! How could this happen?" God declared to Habakkuk that He was going to judge the Babylonians, and He listed five particular areas where His judgment would fall. We come to the fourth of those judgments in Habakkuk 2:15-17,

> *Woe unto him that giveth his neighbour drink, that puttest thy bottle to him, and makest him drunken also, that thou mayest look on their nakedness! Thou art filled with shame for glory:*

103

drink thou also, and let thy foreskin be uncovered: the cup of the LORD's right hand shall be turned unto thee, and shameful spewing shall be on thy glory. For the violence of Lebanon shall cover thee, and the spoil of beasts, which made them afraid, because of men's blood, and for the violence of the land, of the city, and of all that dwell therein.

> *Even when people around us are not living for Christ, we can still be victorious through our personal faith in the Lord Jesus Christ.*

Notice what God said in the fifteenth verse, *"Woe unto him that giveth his neighbour drink, that puttest thy bottle to him."*

Let us consider what the Lord says about liquor. Even when people around us are not living for Christ, we can still be victorious through our personal faith in the Lord Jesus Christ. In this world in which we live, standing for the Lord means going against the grain. As we consider what the Lord says about liquor, we realize that God's opinion is not the popular view of our society.

In the book of Habakkuk, the Lord said that He was going to judge the Babylonians for their use of alcohol. If the Bible is true and if this statement is truly the Word of God, think of those among athletes, models, and movie actors who have advertised liquor and offered it to the people of the world. God's judgment is already pronounced upon this type of behavior. These people, whom the world considers beautiful, have offered their talents and beauty to advertise for the liquor industry. They are all under the certain judgment of God. It is inescapable. They have entered into the inescapable judgment of God by offering liquor to their neighbor.

If you are wondering why I am so serious about this, I am serious about it because of what the Bible declares and what I have witnessed in the lives of others. The first church I pastored was the Greenback Memorial Baptist Church in Greenback, Tennessee. Early on in that pastorate, as I was returning home one evening, just before turning into the little community of Greenback, I saw that an automobile accident had taken place just moments before I arrived. I stopped my car, got out as quickly as I could, and rushed to the scene of the accident. When I arrived, no one had been moved. Two men had been coming over the hill driving north and had struck a man and his family in an oncoming vehicle. The two men in the automobile were unable to stop their vehicle because they could not control it. They were driving under the influence of alcohol. Oddly enough, they did not sustain any serious injuries, but the family they struck suffered greatly.

As we consider what the Lord says about liquor, we realize that God's opinion is not the popular view of our society.

I helped load the father into the rescue squad ambulance as he drew his last breath and died. I later had to tell his family that he was dead. I helped load the mother into an ambulance after seeing that her leg was crushed. She was crippled for life. I helped load a little red-headed boy, whose body was cut and his ankle maimed and crushed. He would be crippled for the rest of his life. We pried up the automobile to retrieve a little preschooler from underneath and then reached back under the wreckage and got his leg which had been severed from his body. I carried it in my lap in the ambulance all the way to the hospital. That little boy would have no leg for the rest of his life, and would grow up without a father because someone wanted to drink a few beers and have a good time.

DRINKING ALCOHOL CAUSES SUFFERING

The Bible says in Habakkuk 2:15, *"Woe unto him that giveth his neighbour drink, that puttest thy bottle to him, and makest him drunken also, that thou mayest look on their nakedness!"*

The word *"woe"* means "judgment and destruction." Drinking alcohol brings suffering. Consider some statistical information I have gathered. One information sheet comes from the third and fourth *Special Reports to the United States Congress on Alcohol and Health.* In this report the medical authorities say that with every drink one shortens his life twenty minutes. They also tell us that there are eleven to seventeen million alcoholics in America. America spends fifty billion dollars a year on alcohol.

We think that we are making money from taxing liquor, that it is a profitable business, but the report to Congress says that alcohol problems cost the American economy an estimated 68.6 billion dollars every year. These are problems that result from people who drink–physical problems, jobs lost, man hours lost, and accidents taking place on the highways. The leading cause of mental retardation among children is alcohol consumption during pregnancy. I say this as kindly as I know how, but a woman is a careless, selfish human being to drink alcohol while carrying a baby.

Nearly twenty thousand people are killed every year on our highways because of alcohol. One person dies every twenty-one minutes in an alcohol-related auto accident. Of course, that does not mean much to us unless someone we know is involved. Eighty-three percent of all fire fatalities are alcohol-related.

Fifty to sixty-eight percent of all drownings are alcohol-related. Up to eighty percent of all suicides are alcohol-related. Forty percent of all fatal industrial accidents are alcohol-related. Eighty-six percent of all murders are alcohol-related. Sixty-five percent of all child abuse is alcohol-related. This same report says that 200,000 Americans die each year, either because of their own consumption of alcohol or someone else's consumption of alcohol. This information can be obtained by anyone who is interested in knowing the truth.

Another report entitled, "The Truth About Beer," is provided by the United Tennessee League because some people think it is alright to have a few beers.

> Approximately fifty percent of all teenagers have tried beer before they enter high school. Ninety percent of all high school graduates have used beer. Peer pressure is great to join the crowd and have a couple of beers. Eighty percent of the teenagers who drink today indicated that their friends also drink.

> Television commercials present a very glamorous picture of beer drinking. Endorsements by highly recognizable former athletes make beer drinking appear to be the macho thing to do. These commercials show young people enjoying the 'good life' with a beer or other alcoholic beverage in hand. In some commercials, beautiful models endorse beer and thus the sex appeal angle is introduced: 'If you want to get a pretty girl, drink a beer.' Television programs consistently depict the drinking of alcohol as an integral part of an attractive and successful life, and in many

programs, alcohol is presented as a way of coping with the problems of life.

And in case you do not know the facts about beer, the article says,

> The alcohol contained in beer is grain alcohol, chemically known as ethyl alcohol. The percentage of alcohol in beer ranges from approximately three percent to eight percent. This may not seem like much alcohol; however, a twelve-ounce can or bottle of beer contains a half ounce of alcohol. This is the same amount of alcohol that you would obtain from other drinks such as a glass of wine filled with natural wine, an average cocktail, an average highball, an average martini, or a shot of one hundred proof whiskey. Approximately sixty percent of the alcohol consumed in the United States is from beer. Clearly, beer is the beverage of choice by Americans. Alcohol is a very powerful drug to which the body can quickly develop both a psychological and physiological dependence. There are at least eleven million alcoholics and perhaps as many as seventeen million alcoholics in America. Many hundreds of thousands of them are teenagers. One out of every ten drinkers becomes addicted to alcohol. Statistics indicate that one out of every two people will be involved in an alcohol-related accident in their lifetime.

You may say, "It's none of my business." If you have never taken a drink, it is still your business because half of us are going to be hurt by someone who is drinking.

This same report states:

> Alcohol is involved in approximately sixty percent of all highway fatalities. In the United States alone, over twenty-five thousand people die and seven hundred fifty thousand injuries occur on American highways each year because of alcohol. Three quarters of a million people are injured because of alcohol each year in America. Three people are killed and eighty people are injured by alcohol every hour in America. On a typical weeknight, one out of every ten drivers is driving under the influence of alcohol.

And one article said, "There are certain hours during the day when they have proven that not only one out of every ten, but three out of every ten drivers are under the influence of alcohol."

Many say that liquor is a disease. Someone has said, "If liquor is a disease, it's the only disease that requires a license to propagate it. It's the only disease that's bottled and sold. It's the only disease that requires outlets to spread it. It's the only disease that is spread by advertising."

Does it do something to you when you see athletes getting their bodies in tremendous condition and then to see that the sporting events are sponsored, for the most part, by beer companies?

A former Prime Minister of England, William Gladstone, frequently distributed this article to his friends:

> Drunkenness expels reason, drowns the memory, distempers the body, diminishes strength, inflames the blood, causes internal and external wounds; it is a witch to the senses; a devil to the soul; a thief to the purse; a beggar's companion; a wife's woe, and children's sorrow.

I remember the night when my youngest son graduated from our Christian school as valedictorian of his class. I was so grateful to the Lord for him. But the night that I watched him graduate, I could not help but recall that we had a lovely couple in the first church I pastored, who had a son the same age as my youngest son. They were in school together. They had planned to graduate the same night. But their son did not graduate. Their son, a few weeks before graduation, took a friend home and was coming back to his home to be in at the proper time that his parents had allotted for him. A man and a woman in an automobile, who had already taken their clothes off in a drunken stupor, were driving down the highway on the wrong side of the road and crashed into the automobile driven by this young man. They killed him instantly. The drunken driver never knew that he struck my young friend.

"Drunkenness...is a witch to the senses; a devil to the soul; a thief to the purse; a beggar's companion; a wife's woe, and children's sorrow."

Drinking liquor causes suffering. The world is suffering for many reasons, but one of the biggest reasons is beverage alcohol–beer, wine coolers, liquor, and all the rest. God is against it because it causes suffering. It could be you or one of your precious children that is the next to be killed.

DRINKING ALCOHOL CAUSES SHAME

The Bible says in Habakkuk 2:15, *"Woe unto him that giveth his neighbour drink, that puttest thy bottle to him, and makest him drunken also, that thou mayest look on their nakedness!"*

God associates drinking with immorality. He ties the two together. If you ever notice the beer commercials, they are promoting an immoral lifestyle. They say, "Live it up!" And the beautiful young bodies that you see will not remain young and beautiful forever because drinking alcohol will cause shame.

I noticed, in my reading, that a famous actor who portrays a constant drinker and philosopher on a television sitcom has had himself admitted into an alcoholics' treatment center. Though he portrays a character that promotes drinking every week on television, he has had to admit himself into an alcoholics' treatment center and has tried to commit suicide on a number of occasions while in that center. I am not against that man, but I am against his sin and what he promotes. If anyone should see it, he should see it. I could go down a list of famous people who have either overdosed, killed themselves, or wrecked and ruined their lives because of their drinking or substance abuse. Drinking brings shame.

Have you ever seen a drunken woman? I remember from my childhood seeing drunken women. Everything that was decent and holy about life was shamefully disgraced as something beautiful turned into something animal-like. These women had no regard for what they did; they had no shame in showing their bodies or using filthy language because of drinking liquor.

The Word of God says in Habakkuk 2:16, *"Thou art filled with shame for glory: drink thou also, and let thy foreskin be uncovered: the cup of the LORD's right hand shall be turned unto thee, and shameful spewing shall be on thy glory."*

What does the last part of verse sixteen mean? It literally means that they would be vomiting on their own glory. He said, "Mighty Babylon, greater than all, you will be vomiting on your own glory." If you will remember from the reading of God's Word in Daniel chapter five, one night the leaders of Babylon were in a drunken stupor and fell to the Medes and Persians.

Many a man has started out handsome, robust, and strong, and many a young lady has started out looking beautiful. Somehow they found their way into a singles' bar or some "club," and the Devil lied to them until everything good was gone. No honor was left. Their honor was given to the cruel, and now all that is left is shame.

I know men and women of means who have destroyed their health; who started drinking with family as young people, and today they are drunkards. Even with all the wealth they possess, they cannot regain what they have lost. Their lives are covered with shame because of drinking.

Heed this warning that the Lord gives us in Hosea 4:6,

> *My people are destroyed for lack of knowledge: because thou hast rejected knowledge, I will also reject thee, that thou shalt be no priest to me: seeing thou hast forgotten the law of thy God, I will also forget thy children.*

You may need to share this with someone someday because God will use His Word to speak to that person. God is speaking here about the leadership of Israel and what happened to them. He rejects them, and I want you to notice why. The Bible continues in verses seven through eleven,

> *As they were increased, so they sinned against me: therefore will I change their glory into shame. They eat up the sin of my people, and they set their heart on their iniquity. And there shall be, like people, like priest: and I will punish them for their ways, and reward them their doings. For they shall eat, and not have enough: they shall commit whoredom, and shall not increase: because they have left off to take*

heed to the LORD. Whoredom and wine and new wine take away the heart.

God says the entire problem came with whoredom and drinking, and He had to reject His own people.

The Bible says in Isaiah 28:7,

But they also have erred through wine, and through strong drink are out of the way; the priest and the prophet have erred through strong drink, they are swallowed up of wine, they are out of the way through strong drink; they err in vision, they stumble in judgment.

In Proverbs 20:1 the Bible says, *"Wine is a mocker, strong drink is raging: and whosoever is deceived thereby is not wise."* You do not know what you have your hands on when you hold a bottle of beer. You do not know what you have your hands on when you hold a glass of wine. You may say, "I know people who can handle it." No, you do not, friend. It just looks as if they can now.

You may ask, "What about wine?" Go with me to New York City, where I spent eight years ministering to people, or any other major city in America, and I will show you the people whose minds are gone. What do we call them? We call them "winos." Why are they called winos? Because the cheap wine that they drink destroys more of the brain cells than any other beverage alcohol. Wine is a mocker. This is what the Bible says.

In Proverbs 23:19-35 the Bible says, *"Hear thou, my son, and be wise, and guide thine heart in the way. Be not among winebibbers; among riotous eaters of flesh."* This means if you have gotten into the company of drinkers, you had better find another crowd.

"For the drunkard and the glutton shall come to poverty: and drowsiness shall clothe a man with rags. Hearken unto thy father that begat thee, and despise not thy mother when she is old." Some may say, "Those old people don't know what they are talking about!" They do know what they are talking about!

> *Buy the truth, and sell it not; also wisdom, and instruction, and understanding. The father of the righteous shall greatly rejoice: and he that begetteth a wise child shall have joy of him. Thy father and thy mother shall be glad, and she that bare thee shall rejoice.*

No mother and father rejoices when their children are in sin, destroying their lives. The Bible says,

> *My son, give me thine heart, and let thine eyes observe my ways. For a whore is a deep ditch; and a strange woman is a narrow pit. She also lieth in wait as for a prey, and increaseth the transgressors among men. Who hath woe? who hath sorrow? who hath contentions? who hath babbling? who hath wounds without cause? who hath redness of eyes? They that tarry long at the wine; they that go to seek mixed wine. Look not thou upon the wine when it is red, when it giveth his colour in the cup, when it moveth itself aright.*

Have you seen the wine-tasters move the wine around and talk about the body and the fragrance of the wine and how beautiful it is? The Bible says not to look at it because,

> *At the last it biteth like a serpent, and stingeth like an adder. Thine eyes shall behold strange women, and thine heart shall utter perverse things. Yea, thou shalt be as he that lieth down in*

the midst of the sea, or as he that lieth upon the top of a mast. They have stricken me, shalt thou say, and I was not sick; they have beaten me, and I felt it not: when shall I awake? I will seek it yet again.

How pitiful! People wake up after being affected by liquor, but when they wake up, they get another drink.

I have seen people beautifully dressed enter into a place and come out acting like, excuse me, the worse kind of harlot that ever lived. What changed their behavior? Alcohol. I have seen mighty strong men brought down by alcohol. Drinking alcohol causes shame.

DRINKING ALCOHOL CAN BE STOPPED

The Lord Jesus Christ can enable a person to stop drinking. This is not a matter that one can simply fight his way through; he must have God's power. You may say, "I'm going to turn over a new leaf. I'm going to give up the booze. I'll clean out my refrigerator; I'll never take another drink." That will not do it. It is not just turning from the evil; it is turning to the Lord that we need.

I would to God that every man, woman, boy and girl in the world would say, "I'll give my life to the Lord Jesus. I'll ask Him to forgive my sin and by faith trust Him as my Savior." Are you a Christian? Are you truly a Christian? Then may everyone of us say, "By the grace of God, we will live for Christ."

If you do not know Him as your Savior, you should trust Him now. Ask Him to forgive your sin and be your Savior. Living for Christ is a daily matter. You will be strengthened day by day, and with each passing day, God will help you to be stronger to resist temptation. It will be a daily matter, but you can stop.

Every evil in our lives should be treated as if we are living with the Devil himself, and we should say, "God, help me! I won't bring this Devil into my life anymore! God, help me."

> *Every victory in life is won by living consciously in the presence of Jesus Christ.*

Call it "sin" like it is. Call it sin and go to Christ and ask Him to help you. Ask Him to forgive you and help you and He will. Every victory in life is won by living consciously in the presence of Jesus Christ.

This is not just about drinking liquor. The Lord Jesus loves you. He will forgive you for everything you have ever done and come to live in your life. He will give you the Holy Spirit to empower you to do what is right if you will simply trust Him. No one can trust Him for you. Others can pray for you and they can love you, but you must give your heart to Him. May God help you to do this today.

WHAT DOES THE LORD SAY ABOUT LIQUOR?

BIBLE MEMORY VERSES

"For they eat the bread of wickedness, and drink the wine of violence."

Proverbs 4:17

"Wine is a mocker, strong drink is raging: and whosoever is deceived thereby is not wise."

Proverbs 20:1

"He that loveth pleasure shall be a poor man: he that loveth wine and oil shall not be rich."

Proverbs 21:17

"Who hath woe? who hath sorrow? who hath contentions? who hath babbling? who hath wounds without cause? who hath redness of eyes? They that tarry long at the wine; they that go to seek mixed wine. Look not thou upon the wine when it is red, when it giveth his colour in the cup, when it moveth itself aright. At the last it biteth like a serpent, and stingeth like an adder. Thine eyes shall behold strange women, and thine heart shall utter perverse things. Yea, thou shalt be as he that lieth down in the midst of the sea, or as he that lieth upon the top of a mast. They have stricken me, shalt thou say, and I was not sick; they have beaten me, and I felt it not: when shall I awake? I will seek it yet again."

Proverbs 23:29-35

"It is not for kings, O Lemuel, it is not for kings to drink wine; nor for princes strong drink: lest they drink, and forget the law, and pervert the judgment of any of the afflicted."

Proverbs 31:4-5

"Woe unto them that rise up early in the morning, that they may follow strong drink; that continue until night, till wine inflame them!"

Isaiah 5:11

"Woe unto him that giveth his neighbour drink, that puttest thy bottle to him, and makest him drunken also, that thou mayest look on their nakedness!"

Habakkuk 2:15

"Let us walk honestly, as in the day; not in rioting and drunkenness, not in chambering and wantonness, not in strife and envying."

Romans 13:13

"And be not drunk with wine, wherein is excess; but be filled with the Spirit."

Ephesians 5:18

IS THERE COMFORT IN THE SECOND COMING OF JESUS CHRIST?

he most misunderstood doctrine in the Bible is the doctrine of the Second Coming of Jesus Christ. At the same time, the most encouraging doctrine in the Bible is the doctrine of the Second Coming of Jesus Christ. Could it be that the Devil has worked very hard to hide and confuse this great truth because it is such an encouragement to God's people?

Jesus Christ is coming again. All through the Old Testament, God rang a bell for the hope of all His people. It sounded the promise of the coming Messiah.

As New Testament saints in this age of grace, waiting for the sound of the trumpet, we are to look heavenward and be hopeful. When the apostle Paul, under the inspiration of the Spirit of God, wrote I Thessalonians 4:13-18, he said,

But I would not have you to be ignorant, brethren, concerning them which are asleep, that ye sorrow not, even as others which have no hope. For if we believe that Jesus died and rose again, even so them also which sleep in Jesus will God bring with him. For this we say unto you by the word of the Lord, that we which are alive and remain unto the coming of the Lord shall not prevent them which are asleep. For the Lord himself shall descend from heaven with a shout, with the voice of the archangel, and with the trump of God: and the dead in Christ shall rise first: then we which are alive and remain shall be caught up together with them in the clouds, to meet the Lord in the air: and so shall we ever be with the Lord. Wherefore comfort one another with these words.

Notice the word *"comfort"* in verse eighteen. We are encouraged to think of the comfort of His coming. There are many aspects to the Lord's coming. But I want us to consider the comfort of His coming.

This is a day of so much pressure and stress. There seems to be so many more questions than there are answers. There is so much more restlessness than there is peace. God's people must find comfort. The Lord says there is comfort in the coming of Jesus Christ.

Occasionally, when we talk about the Second Coming of the Lord Jesus, people become very frightened. Some children get frightened. Some adults who have been Christians for a long time get frightened. But the Bible says the child of God should be comforted by the truth of Christ's coming. Our hearts should be encouraged by the doctrine of His coming. Our hope is not in the Second Coming of Christ but in the Christ of the Second Coming. We shall see Jesus Christ!

There are certain things about growing up in a home that are comforting, and there are other things that are disturbing. When I was young, it was always comforting to know, especially when we were doing the right things, that our parents were coming home. Also, if it was getting dark, we were comforted by our parents returning home.

> *Our hope is not in the Second Coming of Christ but in the Christ of the Second Coming.*

In this dark hour of human history, we should be comforted by the thought that the Lord Jesus is coming back for His own. We should be encouraged by the fact that at any moment, the trumpet could sound and we could be caught up to be with the Lord Jesus Christ forever.

THE PROMISE OF HIS COMING

When we talk about the character and nature of God, we say there are certain things that we attribute to our Lord. He is immutable; He cannot change. We say that He cannot lie; not that He *will* not lie, but that He *cannot* lie. When you read the Bible, you find that God Himself has promised that He is coming again.

In John chapter fourteen, our Lord is giving the sad news to His disciples concerning His death. He says in John 14:1-3,

> *Let not your heart be troubled: ye believe in God, believe also in me. In my Father's house are many mansions: if it were not so, I would*

*have told you. I go to prepare a place for you.
And if I go and prepare a place for you, I will
come again, and receive you unto myself; that
where I am, there ye may be also.*

Notice the words, *"I will come again."* It does not matter how many times I read that passage, it is always encouraging to me to know that the Lord Jesus Himself said, *"I will come again."*

When we think about our Lord's return, we are not talking about the coming of the Holy Spirit in a new ministry to indwell believers forever on the day of Pentecost. We are not referring to the new birth, when we pray and ask God to forgive our sin and by faith receive Jesus Christ as our Savior. We are talking about the Person of Jesus Christ coming again. This is what the Bible teaches. Our Lord said, *"I will come again."*

In Acts chapter one, our Lord parted with His disciples. He stood on the mount about to ascend, to begin His intercessory ministry for us. The Lord Jesus was caught up in the very presence of His disciples into the clouds. The Bible says in Acts 1:8-9,

*But ye shall receive power, after that the Holy
Ghost is come upon you: and ye shall be
witnesses unto me both in Jerusalem, and in all
Judæa, and in Samaria, and unto the uttermost
part of the earth. And when he had spoken these
things, while they beheld, he was taken up; and
a cloud received him out of their sight.*

The Person of Jesus Christ, from His bodily resurrection, ascended. He was taken up from them in the clouds into heaven.

The Bible says in Acts 1:10-11,

*And while they looked stedfastly toward
heaven as he went up, behold, two men stood by*

> *them in white apparel; which also said, Ye men*
> *of Galilee, why stand ye gazing up into heaven?*
> *this same Jesus, which is taken up from you into*
> *heaven, shall so come in like manner as ye have*
> *seen him go into heaven.*

This is the promise that the Lord Jesus is coming again. And He is coming in like manner. Jesus Christ Himself was caught up in the clouds. Jesus Christ is coming again in the clouds for His church. This is the promise of His coming.

Our Lord tells us why He gave us the third chapter of II Peter. The Bible says in II Peter 3:1, *"This second epistle, beloved, I now write unto you; in both which I stir up your pure minds by way of remembrance."*

In other words, Peter says, "I'm writing this under the inspiration of the Spirit of God. By the very breath of God, I am penning these words to stir you up by way of remembrance. I am calling to your mind things you already know. How do you already know them? Because we have been preaching this, and the Lord Jesus taught us this, and I am going to repeat it to you."

Peter continues in verses two and three,

> *That ye may be mindful of the words which*
> *were spoken before by the holy prophets, and of*
> *the commandment of us the apostles of the Lord*
> *and Saviour: knowing this first, that there shall*
> *come in the last days scoffers, walking after*
> *their own lusts.*

There have always been scoffers. When Christ was on this earth, there were scoffers. An attitude of scoffing about the truth of the Bible has been created through the blasphemous teachings of the anti-God crowd and the lies propagated through the atheistic teaching of evolution and humanism.

What do you really believe in your heart? Can you stand up for what you believe in the midst of people scoffing and ridiculing what the Bible teaches? Do you have God and the things of God so firmly fixed in your heart that you cannot be moved?

Peter, under the inspiration of the Spirit of God, said there are going to be scoffers, *"walking after their own lusts."* They live the way they do for self-gratification.

The Bible says in II Peter 3:4-11,

> *And saying, Where is the promise of his coming? for since the fathers fell asleep, all things continue as they were from the beginning of the creation. For this they willingly are ignorant of, that by the word of God the heavens were of old, and the earth standing out of the water and in the water: whereby the world that then was, being overflowed with water, perished: but the heavens and the earth, which are now, by the same word are kept in store, reserved unto fire against the day of judgment and perdition of ungodly men. But, beloved, be not ignorant of this one thing, that one day is with the Lord as a thousand years, and a thousand years as one day. The Lord is not slack concerning his promise, as some men count slackness; but is longsuffering to us-ward, not willing that any should perish, but that all should come to repentance. But the day of the Lord will come as a thief in the night; in the which the heavens shall pass away with a great noise, and the elements shall melt with fervent heat, the earth also and the works that are therein shall be burned up. Seeing then that all these things shall*

be dissolved, what manner of persons ought ye
to be in all holy conversation and godliness?

In verse four, we read about scoffing concerning the promise of His coming. There are thousands of promises in the Bible, but Peter writes about one promise here. It is the promise that Jesus Christ is coming again. The Bible says concerning His promise, *"The Lord is not slack."* The Bible speaks here of the full phase of His return, even His coming to execute judgment on this unbelieving world. He is not slack concerning His promise.

The Lord Jesus is coming again. It makes a difference in your life if you believe this. It makes a difference in your church if you believe this. It makes a difference in your home if you believe this.

THE PLAN OF HIS COMING

What is going to happen when the Lord Jesus comes? Will the world come to an end? Absolutely not. As Christians, our existence on this earth will be over. Our day of opportunity to serve the Lord is today.

Our day of opportunity to serve the Lord is today.

I have one body in which to serve the Lord. Some day, the Bible says, I shall give an account unto God for the works done in my body. My body identifies me with this world. A new body identifies me with the world to come. God is not finished with this body. It will be planted corruptible and raised incorruptible. We find this taught in the Word of God.

Our Lord will come again. We will be caught up to be with Him at the Rapture of the church. On the earth, seven years of

Tribulation will take place, divided equally into three-and-one-half year periods. The last three-and-one-half years will be the most intense.

At the end of that seven-year period, the Lord Jesus Christ is coming to execute judgment on this unbelieving world, and we are coming with Him. At the Rapture, He is coming *for* us; seven years later, at His revelation, we are coming *with* Him.

> *We are not looking for signs; we are looking for the Savior.*

When Jesus Christ has executed judgment upon this earth, He will rule and reign in a literal kingdom upon the earth for one thousand years. He has promised to rule on the throne of His father David, and the only throne that His father David ever had was an earthly throne. Yes, Jesus Christ is God, eternally existent with God the Father and God the Holy Spirit. But His throne is an earthly throne and that throne will be upon the earth as the Lord Jesus reigns from Jerusalem for one thousand years in the millennial kingdom. And we shall reign with Him.

In this lesson, we are dealing primarily with the Rapture, the thing that sets all of this in motion. We are not looking for signs; we are looking for the Savior. Every Christian will hear the trump of God. We will be caught up to be with the Lord Jesus.

In the brief passage of I Thessalonians chapter four, God tells us the plan, what will take place at the Rapture of the church. He says, "Brethren, I'm writing this so you won't be ignorant."

I Thessalonians 4:13 says, *"But I would not have you to be ignorant, brethren, concerning them which are asleep, that ye sorrow not, even as others which have no hope."*

Do you have hope? Our hope is in the Lord. Verse fourteen says, *"For if we believe that Jesus died and rose again, even so them also which sleep in Jesus will God bring with him."* Once you believe in the bodily resurrection of Jesus Christ, you have no problem with the creation of the world. Once you believe in the bodily resurrection of Jesus Christ, you have no problem with life after death. Once you believe in the bodily resurrection of Jesus Christ, you have no problem believing in a real, literal heaven where we are going to be with our Lord. Once you believe in the bodily resurrection of Jesus Christ, you have no problem believing anything else in the Bible.

How can we sleep in Jesus Christ and also be caught up with Him? When we die, we are separated from our bodies. To be absent from the body is to be present with the Lord.

After someone dies, we fondly remember him by the appearance of his body. We weep at the casket over his body. We are emotional when we look into the face of that body. But the truth is, if we know the Bible, that body is not the one we knew and loved. That is only the tabernacle in which he lived while he was here.

> *Once you believe in the bodily resurrection of Jesus Christ, you have no problem believing anything else in the Bible.*

I cannot explain it all to you, and I am not going to try. But I know that I have a body, and my body will be laid down some day, dead. Tender, loving hands will take my body and prepare it. It will be placed in the earth somewhere waiting for the resurrection of the body. But my soul will not be sleeping. The soul does not sleep. I will be gone to be with God. Only my body will be planted in the earth.

The body is referred to as *"sleeping."* We are set free to be with the Lord Jesus. Whether it is in a hospital room or in an automobile accident, wherever it may be, the moment we take our last breath, if we are children of God, we will go to be with Christ. Although our bodies will be planted in the earth, we who die in Christ will be asleep in the Lord Jesus and will be with Him.

The Bible says the Lord Jesus will bring them with Him. I Thessalonians 4:15 says, *"For this we say unto you by the word of the Lord, that we which are alive and remain unto the coming of the Lord shall not prevent them which are asleep."* This means we will not precede them.

I Thessalonians 4:16 says, *"For the Lord himself shall descend from heaven with a shout, with the voice of the archangel, and with the trump of God: and the dead in Christ shall rise first."* The dead are planted beneath the earth, and they are coming up first. The simple truth is, when they reach the top of the earth, we which are alive are going up together with them that slept.

Verse seventeen says, *"Then we which are alive and remain shall be caught up together with them in the clouds, to meet the Lord in the air: and so shall we ever be with the Lord."*

We do not need to get into a debate about how we are coming out of the earth and what we are going to look like. God will take care of that. We will have a body unlike the molecular structure of this body. That body we shall have someday will be able to walk through walls, like the Lord Jesus walked through closed doors. That body will be called out of the earth, a body incorruptible like our Lord's resurrected body.

The day of deceiving will be over. There will be those whose names may have been on the church role but their names were not in the Lamb's Book of Life. All deception will end.

What a horrible thing to think you could be left behind. Settle your doubts. Make sure of your salvation. Find comfort in the coming of the Lord Jesus, not fear.

The most grand, glorious moment in the life of a child of God is when he sees Jesus Christ. Our last day on this earth shall be our greatest day–the day we see our Savior.

The Bible says in I Thessalonians 4:17, *"Then we which are alive and remain shall be caught up together with them in the clouds, to meet the Lord in the air: and so shall we ever be with the Lord."*

We are so worldly, so fastened to this world, that we have forgotten what glory awaits us. My body will be planted in the earth if I die before He comes. If my loved ones are still here, they will be changed in a moment, in the twinkling of an eye. We will be reunited with them in the air, and we will be together with the Lord forever.

> *The most grand, glorious moment in the life of a child of God is when he sees Jesus Christ. Our last day on this earth shall be our greatest day–the day we see our Savior.*

No wonder God gave the apostle Paul these things to write in I Corinthians 15:51-55,

> *Behold, I shew you a mystery; We shall not all sleep, but we shall all be changed, in a moment, in the twinkling of an eye, at the last trump: for the trumpet shall sound, and the dead shall be raised incorruptible, and we shall be changed. For this corruptible must put on incorruption, and this mortal must put on immortality. So when this corruptible shall have put on incorruption, and this mortal shall have put on immortality, then shall be brought to pass the saying that is written, Death is swallowed up in*

> victory. O death, where is thy sting? O grave, where is thy victory?

Memorize verse fifty-five because this is what we are going to be saying on the day of the coming of the Lord Jesus for His church. Those who are resurrected from the grave will be looking back at the grave and asking, *"O grave, where is thy victory?"*

Those of us who will never taste death, who will be alive when Christ comes, will ask, *"O death, where is thy sting?"* because we never died. What a wonderful plan God has for us as we think of the comfort of His coming!

THE PREPARATION FOR HIS COMING

Jesus Christ is coming, and we need to prepare. We need to be saved, and we need to be faithfully serving Him. It is just that simple.

Do you know Christ as your personal Savior? Have you asked the Lord Jesus to forgive your sin and by faith asked Him to be your Savior? If you have not, pray and receive the Lord Jesus as your Savior today.

Consider how God closes the Bible. Revelation 22:20 says, *"He which testifieth these things saith, Surely I come quickly."* The last promise in the Bible is that Jesus Christ is coming again.

The last prayer in the Bible, in the same verse of Revelation, is a prayer for His return, *"Even so, come, Lord Jesus."*

As a believer, because of the comfort of His coming, you can pray now for His return.

Is There Comfort in the Second Coming of Jesus Christ?

Bible Memory Verses

"Let not your heart be troubled: ye believe in God, believe also in me. In my Father's house are many mansions: if it were not so, I would have told you. I go to prepare a place for you. And if I go and prepare a place for you, I will come again, and receive you unto myself; that where I am, there ye may be also."
John 14:1-3

"And while they looked stedfastly toward heaven as he went up, behold, two men stood by them in white apparel; which also said, Ye men of Galilee, why stand ye gazing up into heaven? this same Jesus, which is taken up from you into heaven, shall so come in like manner as ye have seen him go into heaven."
Acts 1:10-11

"Behold, I shew you a mystery; We shall not all sleep, but we shall all be changed, in a moment, in the twinkling of an eye, at the last trump: for the trumpet shall sound, and the dead shall be raised incorruptible, and we shall be changed."
I Corinthians 15:51-52

"But I would not have you to be ignorant, brethren, concerning them which are asleep, that ye sorrow not, even as others which have no hope. For if we believe that Jesus died and rose again, even so them also which sleep in Jesus will God bring with him. For this we say unto you by the word of the Lord, that we which are alive and remain unto the coming of the Lord shall not prevent them which are asleep. For the Lord himself shall descend from heaven with a shout, with the voice of the archangel, and with the trump of God: and the dead in Christ shall rise first: then we which are alive and remain shall

be caught up together with them in the clouds, to meet the Lord in the air: and so shall we ever be with the Lord. Wherefore comfort one another with these words."

I Thessalonians 4:13-18

"The Lord is not slack concerning his promise, as some men count slackness; but is longsuffering to us-ward, not willing that any should perish, but that all should come to repentance. But the day of the Lord will come as a thief in the night; in the which the heavens shall pass away with a great noise, and the elements shall melt with fervent heat, the earth also and the works that are therein shall be burned up. Seeing then that all these things shall be dissolved, what manner of persons ought ye to be in all holy conversation and godliness, looking for and hasting unto the coming of the day of God, wherein the heavens being on fire shall be dissolved, and the elements shall melt with fervent heat?"

II Peter 3:9-12

"He which testifieth these things saith, Surely I come quickly. Amen. Even so, come, Lord Jesus."

Revelation 22:20

Chapter Eight

WHAT DOES GOD'S WORD SAY ABOUT GOING TO WAR?

hen we look for answers to the things that matter most in life, we do not need to look to men; we need to look to God. When we deal with subjects as serious as the subject of war, let us go to God's Word and see what the Bible has to say. We must not try to twist the Bible to fit our opinions but ask God by His Spirit to teach us what He has declared in His Book.

The Bible says in Romans 13:1-4,

> *Let every soul be subject unto the higher powers. For there is no power but of God: the powers that be are ordained of God. Whosoever therefore resisteth the power, resisteth the ordinance of God: and they that resist shall receive to themselves damnation. For rulers are*

> *not a terror to good works, but to the evil. Wilt*
> *thou then not be afraid of the power? do that*
> *which is good, and thou shalt have praise of the*
> *same: for he is the minister of God to thee for*
> *good. But if thou do that which is evil, be afraid;*
> *for he beareth not the sword in vain: for he is the*
> *minister of God, a revenger to execute wrath*
> *upon him that doeth evil.*

The Bible says in I Peter 2:13-14,

> *Submit yourselves to every ordinance of man*
> *for the Lord's sake: whether it be to the king, as*
> *supreme; or unto governors, as unto them that*
> *are sent by him for the punishment of evildoers,*
> *and for the praise of them that do well.*

In these passages of Scripture, God teaches us something about our submission. In the thirteenth chapter of Romans, note an expression in the fourth verse, *"He beareth not the sword in vain."*

What does God's Word say about going to war? Quite frankly, if we read no other passage in the Bible except this one found in the thirteenth chapter of Romans, we have the answer to this question. *"He beareth not the sword in vain."* This speaks of war.

W. T. Sherman, the Union leader who led the march to the sea, was the man who became famous for saying, "War is hell." War is not hell; hell is hell. But I think we all know what he meant by this expression.

The European nations of the world have entered into over eight thousand treaties of peace in their history. Every one of them was intended to be permanent, but hardly any of them lasted more than two years. There have been fourteen thousand wars in the last five thousand years of human history.

Here are statistics of the number of Americans killed in some of the wars that concern us. Remember each one represents a human being who had family, loved ones, and friends. In our War for Independence, there were 25,324 Americans killed. In the War of 1812, we had 2,260 people killed. In the Civil War on our soil, in the Northern army, there were 363,020 people killed. In the Confederate army, there were 199,110 people killed. In the Spanish-American War, there were 2,893 Americans killed. In World War I, there were 116,708 Americans killed. In World War II, there were 408,306 Americans killed. In the Korean War, there were 54,246 Americans killed. In the Vietnam War, there were 58,219 Americans killed. War is a horrible thing.

I have had the opportunity to drive through the state of Kansas. In Abilene, I stopped at the home and presidential library of Dwight Eisenhower. I found a letter he wrote to his wife Mamie on April 16, 1944, while he was leading our forces in Europe in World War II. He wrote,

> How I wish this cruel business of war could be completed quickly. Entirely aside from longing to return to you (and stay there) it is a terribly sad business to total up the casualties each day— even in an air war—and to realize how many youngsters are gone forever. A man must develop a veneer of callousness that lets him consider such things dispassionately; but he can never escape a recognition of the fact that back home the news brings anguish and suffering to families all over the country. Mothers, fathers, brothers, sisters, wives, and friends must have a difficult time preserving any comforting philosophy and retaining any belief in the eternal rightness of things. War demands real toughness of fiber–not

only in the soldiers that must endure, but in the homes that must sacrifice their best.

I became an adult during the Vietnam War. Many of my buddies went off to that war. A number of men I knew personally, had played with as a boy, and grew into manhood with, were killed in Vietnam, and their remains were shipped back in body bags. It was a horrible experience to pick up the papers each week and look for the names of those from our hometown who had been killed in that war.

When God blessed my wife and me with sons, I thought often because of what we had lived through, that there might come a time when my sons would be called to go and, if need be, give their lives in some war effort engaged in by our country. My children, thus far, have been spared from that.

For many people in some nations of the world, war is not something that comes every generation or two; war is something that is constantly on their minds. We need to know what the Bible has to say about going to war.

GOVERNMENT IS ORDAINED OF GOD

As we read our Bibles, we know that God has established the institutions of the home, the church, and human government.

The Bible says in Genesis 9:6, *"Whoso sheddeth man's blood, by man shall his blood be shed: for in the image of God made he man."* As long as there is sin, there will be war. We have basically two causes for war—the sin of man or the wrath of God.

Government is ordained of God. It is very important to settle this in your mind. There will always be those who have an anarchistic spirit, but we must realize that, to have civilized behavior among human beings, we must have a civilized

government. This government is ordained of God. Because man is a sinner, he must be protected from other men. I feel that I can lie down to sleep at night and know that there is a form of government—local, county, city, state, and national—that will do what is necessary to protect its citizens.

In the Bible passage found in I Peter 2:13-14 the Word of God says,

> *Submit yourselves to every ordinance of man for the Lord's sake: whether it be to the king, as supreme; or unto governors, as unto them that are sent by him for the punishment of evildoers, and for the praise of them that do well.*

In Genesis 9:6, God speaks of shedding blood. The verse says, *"Whoso sheddeth man's blood, by man shall his blood be shed: for in the image of God made he man."* When we talk about taking someone's life, we deal sometimes with the subject of murder and sometimes with the subject of killing. All murder is killing, but not all killing is murder.

As long as there is sin, there will be war.

I will give you one example that will help you understand, and then we are going to take it to a larger aspect. Let us imagine that we follow the clear command of God's Word and say that a government has the right to exercise what we refer to as capital punishment, that there are certain crimes that people commit and for their crimes, they should be put to death. This is clearly taught in the Word of God.

Let us imagine that, as the government executes this particular law, they put a criminal to death. If you work for the institution where that person is put to death, you may be the person employed by that institution to "flip the switch" in that execution process. In doing so, are you a murderer? The answer is "no". Are you a killer? The answer to this question is "no". You are doing what you have been ordered to do by a civilized people determined to protect themselves.

Imagine that you are a police officer who is a practicing Christian. If you are a police officer and you truly know the Lord Jesus as your Savior, you love people who are criminals because you should love everyone. But there may be times when in the line of duty, human beings you love, because of their offense, lose their lives as you are protecting your own life. All of us know of things like this that take place.

> *Individuals do not go to war; nations go to war. Nations send individuals who have been trained to fight in that war.*

We must never forget that government is ordained of God. Some of the people in the church I pastor have sons and daughters in the United States military who are called to serve and carry out what they have been trained to do. They are going at the bidding of their country. They will be called on to do what their country has determined to do.

Individuals do not go to war; nations go to war. Nations send individuals who have been trained to fight in that war. These individuals go into that war as representatives of a country or a nation because that government is ordained of God.

In the Word of God, the book of Daniel is an amazing book that deals with the rise and fall of nations, kingdoms, and world empires. The Bible says in Daniel 2:19-21,

Then was the secret revealed unto Daniel in a night vision. Then Daniel blessed the God of heaven. Daniel answered and said, Blessed be the name of God for ever and ever: for wisdom and might are his: and he changeth the times and the seasons: he removeth kings, and setteth up kings: he giveth wisdom unto the wise, and knowledge to them that know understanding.

Make special note of the expression found in verse twenty-one, which speaks of our Almighty God, *"He removeth kings, and setteth up kings: he giveth wisdom unto the wise, and knowledge to them that know understanding."* God ordained certain principles.

In Romans 9:17 the Bible says, *"For the scripture saith unto Pharaoh, Even for this same purpose have I raised thee up, that I might shew my power in thee, and that my name might be declared throughout all the earth."*

Daniel 2:21 says that God removes and sets up kings. In the New Testament, God's Word says in Romans 9:17 that God raised up Pharaoh that He might show His power and have His name declared through all the earth.

> *We have an all-wise, Almighty, all-knowing God who has ordained government.*

How do you think America came into existence? God raised up our nation. When we say this is a nation blessed of God, it is wonderful that we recognize this; but there are nations that are not blessed and used of God as America is. We must also see the purpose of God in raising up those nations.

We have an all-wise, Almighty, all-knowing God who has ordained government. Government is ordained of God.

GOD'S WORD INSTRUCTS US TO SUBMIT TO THE HIGHER POWERS

The second thing we must realize is that God's Word instructs us to be submissive to these higher powers.

We recognize that government is ordained of God and we think, "What are we to do at this time?" If we read, believe, and obey the Bible, the Bible says that we are to be in obedience to these higher powers. We are to submit ourselves to these higher powers. It is not one citizen or a few citizens, it is the entire nation that goes to war. Not every man will leave his homeland to fight, even if the fight were on our soil, but as a nation, we are to move in obedience to our leaders. This is what God's Word teaches.

> *We are to be in obedience and submission to those whom God has called "the ministers of God."*

Remember that the Bible says in Romans 13:1, *"Let every soul be subject unto the higher powers."* God's Word teaches that we are to be subject to the higher powers. I Peter 2:13 says, *"Submit yourselves to every ordinance of man for the Lord's sake."* We are to be in obedience and submission to those whom God has called "the ministers of God."

When we are asked, "How do you feel about going to war?" we do not need to express how we feel about this. We must respond, "This is what God's Word says about it, and we are going to be obedient to God's Word." This is the way Christians should deal with this issue of war.

In England under the reign of Henry VIII, a certain man was convicted of murder. He was brought before the King of England,

Henry VIII, who gave the man a full pardon. After the man was pardoned, he killed another man and was brought back before Henry VIII. Someone went to Henry VIII and asked, "Are you going to pardon him the second time?" Henry VIII replied, "The first man *he* killed. The second man *I* killed because I pardoned that murderer. He will not be pardoned the second time."

I hope some of these people who want to take it so easy on murderers and all the evil they bring to pass, learn the same lesson that Henry VIII of England learned.

GOING TO WAR IS SOMETIMES THE NECESSITY OF NATIONS

Not only is government ordained of God, not only does God's Word teach that we are to be submissive to higher powers, but going to war is sometimes the necessity of nations. There are times when we must go to war. We find examples of this all through the Bible.

Notice what the Lord Jesus said when speaking to Pilate in the eighteenth chapter of John. The Lord Jesus was talking about kingdoms. Verse thirty-six says, *"Jesus answered, My kingdom is not of this world: if my kingdom were of this world, then would my servants fight, that I should not be delivered to the Jews: but now is my kingdom not from hence."*

We know that our God is coming back to this earth to execute judgment on unbelievers. The Bible says in John 19:9-10,

> *And went again into the judgment hall, and saith unto Jesus, Whence art thou? But Jesus gave him no answer. Then saith Pilate unto him, Speakest thou not unto me? knowest thou not that I have power to crucify thee, and have power to release thee?*

Make note of what the Lord Jesus said to Pilate in verse eleven, *"Thou couldest have no power at all against me, except it were given thee from above: therefore he that delivered me unto thee hath the greater sin."* What Christ said in this passage is not just the truth of His own crucifixion and Pilate's response to it; He was declaring to us the principle concerning what God does in the affairs of nations.

> *There are times when we must defend ourselves.*

There is an interesting passage in the Gospel according to Luke. Any way that you interpret it, you have to come to one conclusion. As our Lord spoke to His disciples, He said in Luke 22:35-36,

> *When I sent you without purse, and scrip, and shoes, lacked ye any thing? And they said, Nothing. Then said he unto them, But now, he that hath a purse, let him take it, and likewise his scrip: and he that hath no sword, let him sell his garment, and buy one.*

He says, "If you don't have a sword, sell your garment and buy one." If you do not want to make war out of this, fine; but you cannot make anything less of it than self-defense. There are times when we must defend ourselves.

There is a time for nations to rise up out of necessity and go to war. It is a moral duty. It is not something that we enjoy doing, but it is a demand that is placed upon nations from time to time in their existence. It is a necessity that nations are called to defend themselves.

We must also remember that war is something God uses in judgment. In Ezekiel chapter fourteen, we find what I believe to

be the most alarming thought in the Bible concerning this subject. The Bible says in verse twenty-one, *"For thus saith the Lord GOD; How much more when I send my four sore judgments upon Jerusalem, the sword, and the famine, and the noisome beast, and the pestilence, to cut off from it man and beast?"* Here God tells us of His four judgments. Notice the very first one, *"the sword."*

> *There is a time for nations to rise up out of necessity and go to war. It is a moral duty.*

We must ask the question, "Are we doing the right and righteous thing as a nation at this moment?" There are times when others commit evil acts toward us. How will God execute judgment on that evil? He could use another nation to execute judgment with the sword. Going to war is sometimes the necessity of nations.

In this closing thought, I feel that I am dealing with the most misunderstood part of this subject of war. I pray that this very delicate subject will not be misunderstood.

The Bible says in Numbers 21:34-35,

> *And the LORD said unto Moses, Fear him not: for I have delivered him into thy hand, and all his people, and his land; and thou shalt do to him as thou didst unto Sihon king of the Amorites, which dwelt at Heshbon. So they smote him, and his sons, and all his people, until there was none left him alive: and they possessed his land.*

In this war that God instructed Moses to be engaged in, were innocent children killed? I do not think we would say the children committed this sin against God and God's people, but these children were put to death in this war.

There is not a man, woman, or child among us who wants one innocent child anywhere in this world to suffer needlessly. I do not believe there is a man in Washington, D.C., or an American soldier in uniform who wants to see one child killed. But if we go to war, children are going to be killed. We are an extremely humane people. We are a peace-loving, free people. We desire the best for each human life.

The Bible teaches that children who have not reached the time of accountability in their lives will be with God if they die.

This world will never be without war until Jesus Christ comes and reigns in perfect peace.

As strange as it sounds, there is a sense in which there is mercy in war for these children if we believe what we say we believe about heaven, earth, and eternity. This is such a difficult thing to talk about because I do not want one child anywhere in this world to die. I know how people are apt to respond when they see things in the media, but these things are a part of war.

I want to live in a warless world, but this world will never be without war until Jesus Christ comes and reigns in perfect peace. What are we to do? Every Christian should be a good citizen. Every Christian should be obedient to the higher powers. Every Christian should understand that going to war is sometimes the necessity of nations in defending the freedoms and the way of life they enjoy. We must pray and seek God's face. We must pray for our president and for those in our armed forces. We need to pray for our enemies. We need to ask God to help us as Christians to speak in a way that is in agreement with the clear teachings we find in the Word of God.

We must back up our president and pray for our nation. At this time more than ever, we must attend church faithfully and seek God's face. We must pray earnestly.

May God help us to understand what He says in His Word about going to war. As we talk about this subject, let us not speak from our feelings only, but from the clear teaching of the Word of God.

WHAT DOES GOD'S WORD SAY ABOUT GOING TO WAR?

BIBLE MEMORY VERSES

"Whoso sheddeth man's blood, by man shall his blood be shed: for in the image of God made he man."

Genesis 9:6

"Daniel answered and said, Blessed be the name of God for ever and ever: for wisdom and might are his: and he changeth the times and the seasons: he removeth kings, and setteth up kings: he giveth wisdom unto the wise, and knowledge to them that know understanding."

Daniel 2:20-21

"Then saith Pilate unto him, Speakest thou not unto me? knowest thou not that I have power to crucify thee, and have power to release thee? Jesus answered, Thou couldest have no power at all against me, except it were given thee from above: therefore he that delivered me unto thee hath the greater sin."

John 19:10-11

"For the scripture saith unto Pharaoh, Even for this same purpose have I raised thee up, that I might shew my power in thee, and that my name might be declared throughout all the earth."

Romans 9:17

"Let every soul be subject unto the higher powers. For there is no power but of God: the powers that be are ordained of God. Whosoever therefore resisteth the power, resisteth the ordinance of God: and they that resist shall receive to themselves damnation. For rulers are not a terror to good works, but to the evil. Wilt thou then not be afraid of the power? do that which is good, and thou shalt have praise of the same: for he is the minister of God to thee for good. But if thou do that which is evil, be afraid; for he beareth not the sword in vain: for he is the minister of God, a revenger to execute wrath upon him that doeth evil."

Romans 13:1-4

"Submit yourselves to every ordinance of man for the Lord's sake: whether it be to the king, as supreme; or unto governors, as unto them that are sent by him for the punishment of evildoers, and for the praise of them that do well."

I Peter 2:13-14

Chapter Nine

IS ABORTION THE KILLING OF THE UNBORN?

We are dealing with a most serious subject–the killing of the unborn. Not only must we come face to face with what God says about this sin, but we must also deal with how God will forgive, cleanse, and help those who have committed this sin.

Abortion is a horrible thing. Since 1973, millions of innocent babies have been killed in America. All those involved in abortion have committed a horrible crime against God and against these innocent, unborn babies.

The Bible says in Psalm 139:13-19,

> *For thou hast possessed my reins: thou hast covered me in my mother's womb. I will praise thee; for I am fearfully and wonderfully made:*

marvellous are thy works; and that my soul knoweth right well. My substance was not hid from thee, when I was made in secret, and curiously wrought in the lowest parts of the earth. Thine eyes did see my substance, yet being unperfect; and in thy book all my members were written, which in continuance were fashioned, when as yet there was none of them. How precious also are thy thoughts unto me, O God! how great is the sum of them! If I should count them, they are more in number than the sand: when I awake, I am still with thee. Surely thou wilt slay the wicked, O God: depart from me therefore, ye bloody men.

According to reliable statistics, over forty-three million unborn children have been aborted since the infamous Supreme Court ruling made on January 22, 1973, referred to as *Roe versus Wade*. In a 1998 article in *The Washington Times*, Brent Bozell reported this number to be "six times the number of Jews that Adolf Hitler had put to death in his concentration camps." For every two babies born in America, another baby dies in an abortion–that is 1.4 million every year, 4,000 every day, one baby every 20 seconds.

> *Abortion is barbaric behavior.*

Every year in America, over 700,000 abortions are performed after nine weeks into the pregnancy. From 1978 to 2001, in the state of Tennessee alone, over 400,000 babies were killed by abortion. What has gone wrong in this country?

Abortion Promotes Killing

There are millions in America who claim to be "pro-choice." They are really pro-abortion, pro-death, pro-killing of the unborn. These abortionists say that abortion is the premature expulsion of the human fetus. They try to make abortion sound as non-violent as possible.

Abortion promotes killing. Abortion is barbaric behavior. One of the key strategies of the so-called "pro-choice" group is to promote the idea that a woman has a right to do with her body as she pleases, that the mother should be able to choose whether or not she wants to have a baby. I will not argue that a woman has the right to choose whether or not to have a baby, but that choice should be made before conception, not after conception.

> *I will not argue that a woman has the right to choose whether or not to have a baby, but that choice should be made before conception, not after conception.*

Abortion Promotes Child Abuse

Abortion promotes child abuse. We were told by the people who worked to legalize abortion in our country, that child abuse would fall to an all-time low if abortion laws were passed. But just the opposite has been found to be true; child abuse has increased. Why not abuse them outside the womb if it is legal to abuse them inside the womb? The attitude that abortion promotes about life and the detrimental effect it has on the human conscience can do nothing but increase the abuse of children.

Abortion Devalues Life

With the epidemic of random killings taking place in our country today, let us ask the criminals, "How can you kill without caring? How can you randomly drive by, point a pistol out the window, fire it at point-blank range, kill innocent bystanders, and think nothing of it? How can you kill someone and think nothing of it simply because you don't like the way a person looks? How can you kill the driver of the car beside you just to get the set of tires from his car?"

> *One of the great sins of any nation is the indifference of the people who stand by and never raise a voice against what is wrong.*

With the bloodstains of millions of babies on our land, we have devalued life. Though I am very opposed to abortion, I will accept some of the blame. We cannot blame the condition of our country simply on the people who are committing the crimes. Much of the blame lies at the feet of silent people who know better and should do better but never raise their voices to speak the truth in love. One of the great sins of any nation is the indifference of the people who stand by and never raise a voice against what is wrong.

Life has been devalued. This is especially difficult because of the fact that abortion is legal but goes against everything God's Word teaches concerning the preciousness of life. These people are not breaking the laws of the land, but they are breaking the law of God.

Let us look at a brief history of the abortion cause. In 1967, the American Law Institute proposed a law that would allow abortion in cases of rape, incest, threat to the life or health of the mother, or a grave defect in the child. Of course, the reporting of pregnancy due to rape has been greatly exaggerated. We are told by the Tennessee Right to Life that only one percent of abortions are performed because of rape or incest. Only three percent are performed due to the mother's health problems. Dr. C. Everett Koop, who was the Surgeon General of the United States for a period of time, has stated that in thirty years of medical practice he never once dealt with a case where the mother's life was endangered because of a child.

Much of the abortion practiced today is because of "defect" in the child. Most of the testing that has been devised to examine babies in the womb has been devised to detect an "imperfect child" in order to have that child aborted if desired. There is a large group of people who raise their voices in this country declaring that it is a burden on society to allow an "imperfect child," a child with some physical or mental defect, to be born. They want to hold parents accountable and accuse them of a crime for allowing such children to come into the world. These people feel that abortion is more than an option; it is a duty.

These people are not breaking the laws of the land, but they are breaking the law of God.

I was with a pastor recently who has a Downs' Syndrome child. The boy is nineteen years old. When the child was born, the doctor said to this pastor and his wife, "If you choose to give birth, we don't want you to ever see the child. We want you to walk out of the hospital, never look at the child, and we will take care of him. There are homes and places for children like this. You never have to look at this child, never have to be with this child, and never need to get attached to this child." The pastor said, "We want to keep him because God has given us this child."

I met their handsome nineteen-year-old son. One of the most pleasant experiences I have had with a young person was the experience I enjoyed in fellowship with that young man as I witnessed the love and kindness he showed to me and to his parents. The lives of many have been blessed from this child's life.

> *The conscience of our nation has been seared.*

In 1969, the National Association for the Repealed Abortion Laws formed and laid the groundwork for abortion on demand. Bernard Nathanson and Betty Freeden gave leadership to the passing of that law.

On July 1, 1970, New York governor Nelson Rockefeller signed a law allowing licensed physicians in his state to perform abortions through the twenty-fourth week of pregnancy. New York City became the abortion capital for America.

In 1972, Jane Roe filed a suit to overturn a Texas law prohibiting her from having an abortion. The court ruled against her wish because her life was not in danger. In 1973, the United States Supreme Court ruled the Texas court decision unconstitutional, canceling laws against abortion in all fifty states.

At the same time, *Doe versus Bolton* had other abortion-limiting provisions ruled unconstitutional. Thus, every restriction against abortion on demand was removed.

One month after the *Roe versus Wade* decision, the pro-abortion faction petitioned the federal courts to order city and state hospitals to make no charge to the poor, and to require that state and federal governments fund abortions for the poor as a part of Medicaid. Because of that ruling, abortion has been used as a method of birth control just as some contraceptive measures.

In 1979, the Supreme Court declared a Massachusetts law unconstitutional that required unmarried minor girls to get the approval of their parents before obtaining a legal abortion. The court said, "Every minor must have the opportunity, if she so desires, to go directly to a court without first consulting and notifying her parents." Many in authority are doing everything possible for young girls to get an abortion without the permission of their parents.

Something has gone terribly wrong in this country. Millions are promoting an action that the Bible clearly says is sinful. Can you imagine the thousands of innocent babies killed every day? The conscience of our nation has been seared.

Early on, the general public was outraged by the practice of abortion. Now, the tide has turned and the shame is gone. If we will take human life in the dawn of its existence, we will take human life in the twilight of its existence. It will not be long until it is unsafe to be elderly or to have something seriously wrong physically.

> *Early on, the general public was outraged by the practice of abortion. Now, the tide has turned and the shame is gone. If we will take human life in the dawn of its existence, we will take human life in the twilight of its existence.*

We need to be shocked into the realization of what is happening in our world. In a book by Cal Thomas entitled *The Death of Ethics,* Mr. Thomas shares a survey that was taken in T. C. Williams High School located in Alexandria, Virginia. He says, "This is a wealthy, suburban area, just outside of Washington, D.C. The school district decided to establish a school-based clinic." By the way, the school-based clinic is one of the fastest growing franchises in America. Thomas continues,

> As do the other school districts in the country, a majority of the Alexandria school board and local politicians believe that making birth control devices available to teenagers, who must still bring a note from home for the school administrator to give them aspirin, will reduce the number of unwanted pregnancies and venereal diseases.

Mr. Thomas says that they do not have to bring a note from home to get abortion counseling. They do not have to bring a note from home to get contraceptives. They do not have to bring a note from home to be counseled by a guidance counselor to go to Planned Parenthood and get an abortion. But they do have to bring a note from home to get an aspirin. What an educational system!

In an article for *The Washington Post,* Mr. Thomas wrote of the amoral attitudes of many modern teenagers who see nothing wrong with having sex and being outspoken about it. He says they are "oblivious to any man-made or God-made standards. This amorality is worse than immorality. With immorality, there is a standard to which one can appeal to bring back the errant. With amorality, no one acknowledges the existence of any kind of standard at all."

My sociology professors in college taught about amorality and immorality. Immorality says, "Here is a moral standard. Breaking this moral standard is an immoral thing to do."

We speak now of an amoral society–having no moral standards. An amoral society says, "Whatever you want to do with your life, your body, and your mind is your business." We will not be able to govern a nation that has lost its moral foundation.

An honor student at the same high school in Alexandria said,

> There is a feeling that it is okay for us to have sex because we are educated and know what is going on. We are not going to get pregnant and burden society with unwanted children. We are going to college. We have a future. If we do slip up, we will just get an abortion.

LIFE BEGINS WITH CONCEPTION

Let us establish some things from the Word of God. First, life begins with conception. There is no room for doubt about this as we read the Bible. The expression in Psalm 139:13 says, *"...in my mother's womb."*

During my college days, I learned that each cell in the human body contains forty-six chromosomes, except for one cell, the cell that is used in reproduction. The mother's offering to that reproduction contains twenty-three chromosomes. The father's cell for that reproduction also contains twenty-three chromosomes. When there is conception, when the egg and sperm unite, a one-cell life is developed. Frankly, aside from the nourishment of the mother, that life is independent of the mother and father. Now it is one cell with forty-six chromosomes—twenty-three from the mother and twenty-three from the father. In reality, a father can say that this is just as much his baby as the mother can say it is her baby.

When a woman starts talking about choosing to abort, she should have made a choice before conception about whether or not she wanted a child and whether or not she was going to engage in activity that would produce a child. The responsible position is before conception, but she is still responsible to care for that living being after conception. Life begins with conception.

In the first chapter of Jeremiah, God speaks to the prophet in verse four,

> *Then the word of the LORD came unto me, saying, Before I formed thee in the belly I knew thee; and before thou camest forth out of the womb I sanctified thee, and I ordained thee a prophet unto the nations.*

When does life begin? Life begins with conception. This is clearly taught in the Word of God.

CONCEPTION IS A GIFT FROM GOD

The ability to reproduce, to have a child, is a gift from God. There are three ways in which people have entered the human race. In the beginning we find direct creation. Adam and Eve were created by the Lord and placed in the Garden. Then, there is what we refer to as "natural birth." This is how all of us arrived on planet earth. Of course, this is no less a miracle than what happened in the Garden of Eden. Then there is the Lord Jesus Christ who was born of a virgin. The Lord Jesus Christ is the only One who ever came to earth by virgin birth.

Conception has always been recognized as a gift from God. In Genesis chapter four, Adam and Eve were placed in the world, and they were given the ability and the responsibility to reproduce. The Bible says in Genesis 4:1, *"And Adam knew Eve his wife; and she conceived, and bare Cain, and said, I have gotten a man from the LORD."*

My wife has given birth to two children. I can remember how excited I was when my wife announced to me that she was going to have those children. I can remember how we watched the development of those children. We knew when they started kicking, and we were so excited when the heartbeat could be heard. We knew that there was life there and that God had blessed us. The Bible says in Psalm 127:3, *"Lo, children are an heritage of the LORD: and the fruit of the womb is his reward."* We recognized that conception was a gift from God.

From a book entitled, *Before It's Too Late,* we find the following:

> The Supreme Court has ruled that abortion, even abortion on demand, is an American freedom. But we don't call it abortion anymore. We call it 'post-conceptive fertility control.' Feminists call it 'voluntary miscarriage' and 'every woman's right.'

The Supreme Court of the United States has made it a law that anywhere in this country, for any reason or for no reason at all, one can take that life. Since life is a gift from God, think about how people are accountable to God for those decisions. They are accountable to God for the millions of innocent babies who have been killed. The blood of these babies stains the hands of parents who choose abortion and of people who perform abortions in this country.

STAND WHERE GOD STANDS ON THIS ISSUE

On this issue, as on every issue, we need to stand where God stands. This is an issue where there is absolutely no middle ground.

God's Word deals with this subject. It is our responsibility to declare the whole counsel of God just as Paul stated to the Ephesian elders, *"For I have not shunned to declare unto you all the counsel of God"* (Acts 20:27).

If a man will not preach what the Bible says, fearing God and not fearing people, he should not be in the ministry. The Bible clearly teaches that the unborn child is a human being. We must protect the lives of these unborn children.

> *Of course, the greatest work we do is the work of winning lost souls to Christ and teaching them from God's Word how to live the Christian life. The person who believes the Lord Jesus Christ and follows Him will not choose to have an abortion.*

Millions say, "It's a matter of choice." Whose choice is it? It is impossible to ask the babies whether or not they want to be aborted. We have not pleaded the cause of the unborn as we should have. We have not provided Christian alternatives for broken-hearted parents and daughters as we should have. There should be homes in our churches that are open for expectant girls to live in, in order to provide natural birth for these children. We should be more earnestly engaged in good Christian ministries that are fighting this awful sin and trying to provide the right alternatives for young people.

Of course, the greatest work we do is the work of winning lost souls to Christ and teaching them from God's Word how to live the Christian life. The person who believes the Lord Jesus Christ and follows Him will not choose to have an abortion.

When I started researching this matter, I almost became physically ill over the means that are used to abort children. Gary Bergel, the author of the pamphlet "Abortion in America," describes some of these most common methods of abortion being practiced in this country.

SUCTION METHOD

One type of abortion method used is called suction abortion. "This is the most commonly used method for early pregnancies. In this technique, which was pioneered in Communist China, a powerful suction tube is inserted through the cervix into the womb. The body of the developing baby and the placenta are torn to pieces and sucked into a jar." This is as violent as it sounds.

CURETTE METHOD

Another type of abortion is curette abortion. "This method is most often used in the first thirteen weeks of pregnancy. A tiny, hoe-like instrument, the curette, is inserted into the womb through the dilated cervix, its natural gateway. The abortionist then scrapes the wall of the uterus, cutting the baby's body into pieces. This method is now used less frequently than suction." Using this particular method, at times the abortionist is not able to get the head out, and he has to take his own hand and crush the little baby's skull into small pieces to remove it.

SALT POISONING

The next method is salt poisoning. "This method is generally used after thirteen weeks of pregnancy. A long needle is inserted through the mother's abdomen, and a strong salt solution is injected directly into the amniotic fluid that surrounds the child. The salt is swallowed and 'breathed' and slowly poisons the baby, burning his skin as well. The mother goes into labor about a day later and expels a dead, grotesque, shriveled baby. Some babies have survived this 'salting out' and have been born alive."

CESAREAN SECTION

There is also a cesarean section abortion. "This method is used in the last trimester of pregnancy. The womb is entered by surgery through the wall of the abdomen. The tiny baby is removed and allowed to die by neglect or is sometimes killed by a direct act." Many times in this particular type of abortion, the baby lies on the table, moves about, and cries for someone to help him until he dies.

CHEMICAL ABORTION

The next method is chemical abortion. We are told that this is one of the newer forms of abortion. Doctors use chemicals developed into a hormone-like compound which is "injected or otherwise applied to the muscle of the uterus, causing it to contract intensely, thereby pushing out the developing baby. Babies have been decapitated during these abnormal contractions. Many have been born alive." The side effects to the mother are numerous because of this contorting of the body and the trauma from this type of abortion. A number of mothers have died from cardiac arrest from the compounds that were injected.

PARTIAL BIRTH

By now, most everyone is familiar with the horrors of the partial-birth abortion method. According to an article published by the Concerned Women of America, the abortionist "uses forceps to deliver the entire baby except for the head. At this point, the abortionist uses blunt surgical scissors, or a tracer, to stab the baby at the base of the skull. He then inserts a vacuum tube and sucks the child's brains out. Then he can collapse the skull and pull the dead body through the cervical opening."

THE ABORTION PILL

Of course, there is also the RU-486 abortion, commonly known as the "abortion pill." This method is also described by the Concerned Women of America. "An RU-486 abortion takes place in four visits to the doctor. During the first visit, the woman undergoes a pregnancy test, blood test, pelvic exam and often an ultrasound exam. RU-486 is only effective during the first forty-nine days after conception. At the second visit, the woman takes three RU-486 pills. This anti-progesterone prevents the endometrium (lining of the uterus) from providing progesterone to the unborn child, which is necessary for its nourishment. Thus, the unborn child starves to death. At the third visit, the woman receives a drug that induces cramping in order to expel the dead child from her body. The fourth visit occurs about a week later to ensure the abortion is complete and to monitor the woman's bleeding. If the abortion is not successful, the woman undergoes a surgical abortion."

EMERGENCY CONTRACEPTION

Both oral contraceptives and the intra uterine device may be used as "emergency contraceptives" when they are used shortly after unprotected intercourse to abort a possible pregnancy.

The same effect as using the RU-486 can be caused by using legally prescribed oral contraceptives. Depending on the brand, two to five pills taken twice (twelve hours apart) can be used within 72 hours of unprotected intercourse to abort a possible pregnancy. The intra uterine device may also be implanted up to eight days after unprotected intercourse to abort a possible pregnancy.

We do not need to wonder where God stands on this. Think about your babies and your grandbabies. Think about how much you love them, how much you love to see them, hold them, and kiss them. Think about their bright faces. Think about their laughter, their joy, and their smiles. What is taking place in this country should awaken us! One third of the children conceived in America will be killed while in their mother's womb.

Most of us who have watched any news on this subject have heard or seen the story of the little baby whose arm was torn off in an attempted abortion procedure. The baby lived to be born with one arm.

> *One third of the children conceived in America will be killed while in their mother's womb.*

Who will rise up and defend these innocent children? Their defenders must come from those whose hearts have been stirred by God and who are willing to let their voices be heard.

A tidal wave of awful guilt is sweeping across this country. It is almost impossible to deal with this heavy load of guilt. We are a guilty land, a land full of guilty professionals. There is an awful load of guilt in mothers' hearts and in young girls' hearts. Some people are even losing their minds because of this guilt.

As a nation, we are not at a crossroads, but near the end of the road. Abortion is only one sign of the moral ruin of our nation. If you are ever going to be a praying Christian, be a praying Christian now. If you are ever going to be a faithful Christian, be a faithful Christian now. If you are ever going to be a giving Christian, be a giving Christian now.

When you and I complain about what we do not have, where we cannot go, and what we cannot enjoy, may we hear the cries of the millions of innocent children who have never had an opportunity to live outside the womb.

We need to be somewhere on our faces praying for our nation. Be sure you stand where God stands on this. May God help us.

If you are reading this and you have never placed your faith in Jesus Christ for forgiveness of sin and for salvation, trust Him now. His Word says in Romans 10:13, *"For whosoever shall call upon the name of the Lord shall be saved."*

For more information on the development of unborn children, see "The Chronology of a New Life" in the Appendix.

IS ABORTION THE KILLING OF THE UNBORN?

BIBLE MEMORY VERSES

"And Adam knew Eve his wife; and she conceived, and bare Cain, and said, I have gotten a man from the LORD."

Genesis 4:1

"And he lifted up his eyes, and saw the women and the children; and said, Who are those with thee? And he said, The children which God hath graciously given thy servant."

Genesis 33:5

"Lo, children are an heritage of the LORD: and the fruit of the womb is his reward."

Psalm 127:3

"For thou hast possessed my reins: thou hast covered me in my mother's womb. I will praise thee; for I am fearfully and wonderfully made: marvellous are thy works; and that my soul knoweth right well. My substance was not hid from thee, when I was made in secret, and curiously wrought in the lowest parts of the earth. Thine eyes did see my substance, yet being unperfect; and in thy book all my members were written, which in continuance were fashioned, when as yet there was none of them."

Psalm 139:13-16

"Then the word of the LORD came unto me, saying, Before I formed thee in the belly I knew thee; and before thou camest forth out of the womb I sanctified thee, and I ordained thee a prophet unto the nations."

Jeremiah 1:4-5

WHAT IS THE IMPORTANCE OF MODESTY AND IDENTITY?

 ur God created a world of men and women. The Word of God says in Genesis 1:27, *"So God created man in his own image, in the image of God created he him; male and female created he them."* Notice carefully what the Bible says in the very first book of the Bible, *"Male and female created he them."*

The Bible says in I Timothy 2:1-10,

> *I exhort therefore, that, first of all, supplications, prayers, intercessions, and giving of thanks, be made for all men; for kings, and for all that are in authority; that we may lead a quiet and peaceable life in all godliness and honesty. For this is good and acceptable in the sight of God our Saviour; who will have all men*

to be saved, and to come unto the knowledge of the truth. For there is one God, and one mediator between God and men, the man Christ Jesus; who gave himself a ransom for all, to be testified in due time. Whereunto I am ordained a preacher, and an apostle, (I speak the truth in Christ, and lie not;) a teacher of the Gentiles in faith and verity. I will therefore that men pray every where, lifting up holy hands, without wrath and doubting. In like manner also, that women adorn themselves in modest apparel, with shamefacedness and sobriety; not with broided hair, or gold, or pearls, or costly array; but (which becometh women professing godliness) with good works.

Make note of the expression *"modest apparel."* God's Word speaks of modesty, but it also speaks of identity. The Bible says that God created male and female. The subject we must address is modesty and identity—not simply modesty, but modesty and identity.

The definition of *modesty* is "behaving according to a standard of what is proper or decent and pure, especially not displaying one's body." Modesty is based on the idea that God has an order for all things. Everything must be done decently and in order.

There are some people who have a problem with modesty. There are people who do not dress in a modest or orderly way. They do not dress in a decent, pure way. They do not avoid lewdness. As a matter of fact, we live in a nation that is undressing in public.

Not long ago, I was seated on a plane beside a man from Europe. As we talked, I found out that he was a European government employee who was visiting America. I asked him,

"What are your observations of our country?" This man was not a Christian. He was a visitor to our land, and this was the first thing out of his mouth, "I don't know what you do for a living, but I want to tell you, I have never seen as much nakedness as I have seen in this country." This man from Europe, of all places, made this observation that we are living in a land where there is much nakedness. He saw the immodesty of our land.

The immodest person wears clothing that calls attention to the sexual zones of his or her body. His or her clothing is immodest. This leads to lewdness. It is not decent and pure. You may even find a young lady who is wearing a type of dress that calls attention to the sexual zones of her body. This is immodesty.

> *Modesty is based on the idea that God has an order for all things.*

From a survey done on thousands of eighteen-year-olds, they reported that seven out of every ten eighteen-year-old girls say that they are not virgins. They reported that eight out of every ten eighteen-year-old boys say that they are not virgins. This is staggering to think about. Something very sad has happened to a nation that undresses in public.

Robert Bork, a decent, God-fearing man, has written a book entitled *Slouching Towards Gomorrah*. It is a book about the moral decay in America. In one chapter of his book, he addresses the radical feminist movement. He explains that the radical feminists have redefined the sexes. He says,

> In feminist jargon, 'sex' is merely biological while 'gender' refers to roles and is claimed to be 'socially constructed,' which means that everything about men and women, other than their reproductive organs, can be altered by changes in the social and cultural environment.

One of the major implications of this view is that human sexuality has no natural form but is culturally conditioned. Radical feminists concede that there are two sexes, but they usually claim there are five genders. Though the list varies somewhat, a common classification is men, women, lesbians, gays, and bisexuals. Thus heterosexuality, being socially constructed, is no more 'natural' or desirable than homosexuality.

We must also consider the issue of identity. Under normal conditions we should be able to recognize when we see a person in public whether that person is a man or a woman. There should be no problem recognizing a person for his or her identity. Young men should look like young men. They should dress and behave like young men. Women should look like ladies. The problem may not be modesty as we normally consider modesty, but rather identity. So we must deal with modesty and identity. You must keep your identity and clothe yourself modestly. This is God's design for our lives. The issues of modesty and identity must be faced, especially in this generation. As a matter of fact, one of the great issues facing this generation is this issue of identity.

Men are to have humility and boldness. Humility without boldness produces an effeminate man. Boldness without humility produces a destructive man.

The absence of manhood is easily seen today. Have you thought about the number of children today without a father in the home? In America, according to the Attorney General of the United States, one third of all children conceived will be aborted; one third of all children conceived will be born out of wedlock; and only one third of all children conceived will have a mother and a father in the home. Something has happened to manhood. Men are to have humility and boldness. Humility without boldness produces an effeminate man. Boldness without humility produces a destructive man.

GOD HAS SET A HIGH, HOLY STANDARD FOR HIS PEOPLE

When we come to the book of Leviticus chapter eighteen, we find what the Lord says about His people being identified as the people of God. They are to be a testimony and a witness to other people. He gives certain high, holy standards for His people.

The Bible says in Leviticus 18:1-25,

> *And the LORD spake unto Moses, saying, Speak unto the children of Israel, and say unto them, I am the LORD your God. After the doings of the land of Egypt, wherein ye dwelt, shall ye not do: and after the doings of the land of Canaan, whither I bring you, shall ye not do: neither shall ye walk in their ordinances. Ye shall do my judgments, and keep mine ordinances, to walk therein: I am the LORD your God. Ye shall therefore keep my statutes, and my judgments: which if a man do, he shall live in them: I am the LORD. None of you shall approach to any that is near of kin to him, to uncover their nakedness: I am the LORD. The nakedness of thy father, or the nakedness of thy mother, shalt thou not uncover: she is thy mother; thou shalt not uncover her nakedness. The nakedness of thy father's wife*

shalt thou not uncover: it is thy father's nakedness. The nakedness of thy sister, the daughter of thy father, or daughter of thy mother, whether she be born at home, or born abroad, even their nakedness thou shalt not uncover. The nakedness of thy son's daughter, or of thy daughter's daughter, even their nakedness thou shalt not uncover: for theirs is thine own nakedness. The nakedness of thy father's wife's daughter, begotten of thy father, she is thy sister, thou shalt not uncover her nakedness. Thou shalt not uncover the nakedness of thy father's sister: she is thy father's near kinswoman. Thou shalt not uncover the nakedness of thy mother's sister; for she is thy mother's near kinswoman. Thou shalt not uncover the nakedness of thy father's brother, thou shalt not approach to his wife: she is thine aunt. Thou shalt not uncover the nakedness of thy daughter in law: she is thy son's wife; thou shalt not uncover her nakedness. Thou shalt not uncover the nakedness of thy brother's wife: it is thy brother's nakedness. Thou shalt not uncover the nakedness of a woman and her daughter, neither shalt thou take her son's daughter, or her daughter's daughter, to uncover her nakedness; for they are her near kinswomen: it is wickedness. Neither shalt thou take a wife to her sister, to vex her, to uncover her nakedness, beside the other in her life time. Also thou shalt not approach unto a woman to uncover her nakedness, as long as she is put apart for her uncleanness. Moreover thou shalt not lie carnally with thy neighbour's wife, to defile thyself with her. And thou shalt not let any

*of thy seed pass through the fire to Molech,
neither shalt thou profane the name of thy God:
I am the LORD. Thou shalt not lie with mankind,
as with womankind: it is abomination. Neither
shalt thou lie with any beast to defile thyself
therewith: neither shall any woman stand before
a beast to lie down thereto: it is confusion.
Defile not ye yourselves in any of these things:
for in all these the nations are defiled which I
cast out before you: and the land is defiled:
therefore I do visit the iniquity thereof upon it,
and the land itself vomiteth out her inhabitants.*

Verses one and two of chapter nineteen declare, *"And the
LORD spake unto Moses, saying, Speak unto all the
congregation of the children of Israel, and say unto them, Ye
shall be holy: for I the LORD your God am holy."* A holy God
demands a holy people. God has set a high, holy standard for
His people.

Our standard is not the world's standard. Our standard is to
be what God has said. When are Christian people going to learn
that we do not establish our standards from the standards the
world has set for themselves?

In the eighteenth chapter of Leviticus, notice how many
times God talks about nakedness. After there is nakedness,
every sexual barrier is broken down so that anything goes.

Madonna, the rock performer turned actress, said, "We've
broken all the rules. There are no rules left to break. All that is left
for us to do is to start over, make new rules, and then break them."

Think about the unworthy heroes of the world for this
generation. Think of the standards they are setting. There must
be people in this generation who will say, "We are God's

children. We are God's people. We've been redeemed by the blood of Jesus Christ. God has set a high, holy standard for us, and the standard God has set for us is not the world's standard. We do not think that by being just a step better than the world we are pleasing God."

Think about the unworthy heroes of the world for this generation.

God has placed us in this world to live by a high, holy standard. This separation to God and from the world is not the enemy of evangelism; it is the essential of evangelism. There must be a difference in our lives if we are going to make a difference with our lives.

Everything I do outwardly should come out of a desire to live a holy life. Nothing I do on the outside makes me a spiritual person. No activity makes me a spiritual person. Dressing a certain way does not make me a spiritual person. The desire to dress modestly, to be identified as a man, and to hold God's standard as the standard for my life comes out of a desire to live a holy life and walk with God.

Not long ago, I heard a man preaching on the radio. He was preaching a series of sermons entitled "Disciplines That Produce Godliness." I thought to myself, "It is not discipline that produces godliness. It is godliness, following after God, that produces discipline." The reason so many people have no discipline in life is that they are not pursuing the Lord Jesus Christ.

If all we attempt to do is start on the outside and try to straighten everyone out, we are failing. Living the Christian life must start in the heart with our devotion to Jesus Christ. We must have a heart for God. God has set a high, holy standard for His people.

GOD MAKES A SEPARATION OF THE SEXES

The second thing I want you to notice is that God makes a separation for the sexes. Deuteronomy 22:5 is a verse that is not referred to often today because people are almost afraid to use it. The Word of God says, *"The woman shall not wear that which pertaineth unto a man, neither shall a man put on a woman's garment: for all that do so are abomination unto the LORD thy God."* In other words, there is a difference between a man and a woman.

I have had the privilege to travel around the world—Asia, Africa, Europe, South America, Central America, and different islands of the sea. I have found that when you try to locate a restroom, there are certain symbols that are used. If you are trying to find a men's restroom, there is a certain international symbol on the door. If you are trying to find a ladies' restroom, there is a certain international symbol on the door. On the ladies' door, there is a figure with a skirt. On the men's door, there is a figure with a pair of pants. These symbols reflect modesty and identity.

> *Everything I do outwardly should come out of a desire to live a holy life.*

Something is wrong in a world where one cannot identify men from women. Who is going to set the standard? God has already set the standard, and He expects His people to be obedient. God's people must realize that the Lord has made a separation of the sexes.

THERE IS A DIFFERENCE BETWEEN ATTRACTION AND SEXUALITY

In the closing part of the ninetieth Psalm, we find that there is a difference between attraction and sexuality. People so often confuse these two.

In Psalm 90:17 the Bible says, *"And let the beauty of the LORD our God be upon us: and establish thou the work of our hands upon us; yea, the work of our hands establish thou it."*

The Bible says in I Peter 3:3-4,

> *Whose adorning let it not be that outward adorning of plaiting the hair, and of wearing of gold, or of putting on of apparel; but let it be the hidden man of the heart, in that which is not corruptible, even the ornament of a meek and quiet spirit, which is in the sight of God of great price.*

We are to have beauty in the inner man. There is a world of difference between what is identified as sexual attraction and real attraction. Any woman can dress immodestly. Any woman can dress in such a way that she takes off enough of her clothes to call attention to her body. It takes nothing decent, right, pure, and nothing of character to do that. But if we consider that to be attractive, then we have missed the whole point.

Real attractiveness is the beauty of the inner man. Many men have been attracted to something physical only to find out in a matter of days, weeks, or months that it is not an enduring attractiveness. It is staggering that more than half of the people in this country who get married have their marriages end in divorce. There should be a beauty inside, the beauty of the Lord upon us, the beauty of the inner man.

My wife and I have been married for over thirty-six years. She is a beautiful lady. I think she was the most beautiful girl in our high school, inwardly and outwardly. I am attracted to her. She is gorgeous. But as beautiful as she is on the outside, she is even more beautiful on the inside.

Many people have tried to make themselves attractive on the outside and they have used sexuality to do so, but they have never developed the inner man. They have violated the principles of modesty and identity and what is orderly in God's Word. It will not work. The foundation they think they are building on is not a foundation at all. It will crumble like sand, and their hearts will be broken because of it.

Real attractiveness is the beauty of the inner man.

This is the first generation of Christians that will dress so immodestly yet still dare to call themselves Christian. Know the difference between attractiveness and sexuality, and allow this to make a difference in your life.

THE BLUSH IS GONE IN THIS GENERATION

The blush is gone from so many in this generation. In Jeremiah 6:15-16 the Bible says,

> *Were they ashamed when they had committed abomination? nay, they were not at all ashamed, neither could they blush: therefore they shall fall among them that fall: at the time that I visit them they shall be cast down, saith the LORD. Thus saith the LORD, Stand ye in the ways, and see, and ask for the old paths, where is the good way,*

and walk therein, and ye shall find rest for your souls. But they said, We will not walk therein.

The Bible also says in Jeremiah 8:12,

Were they ashamed when they had committed abomination? nay, they were not at all ashamed, neither could they blush: therefore shall they fall among them that fall: in the time of their visitation they shall be cast down, saith the LORD.

The Bible says that this nation could no longer blush. How did we become a people who have lost our blush?

Allow me to give you an example. A little girl is dressed in a way that more of her body is showing than should show. She feels a little uncomfortable going out of the house that way, but Mommy thinks she looks good. Then she slips on a piece of clothing that exposes the midriff. She has never gone out in public this way. Her parents may have seen her like this, but she has never gone out in public showing this much flesh. She is a little embarrassed and she tries to pull down on the top. But other girls are doing the same thing, so why should she care?

She is embarrassed by it, but after a while she gets used to it. She gets used to other parts of her body showing that should be covered. Her dress gets skimpier and skimpier. She gets older and more developed, but she is already used to showing parts of her body so she does not care anymore.

Standards of decency, purity, modesty, and identity are fading. She once pulled on her little dress to make it longer and tried to cover her body. Now she wants to wear clothing that accentuates the wrong things. She wants to wear things that are really too small for her because she wants to accentuate the sexual zones of her body. She wants to wear clothing as revealing as she possibly can just to try to infatuate the minds of people. It makes no difference whose heads she turns, men or women, just so she turns them. She does not care anymore because her blush is gone.

This is what we see happening on the outside, but what has happened on the inside? God gave her a conscience. Her conscience used to cry out, "That's not right. Don't do that! You should have on more clothes. You should look different." But she does not want to hear that conscience, so she tries to silence it. She does not want to go anywhere where people are talking about things that make that conscience continue to cry out. She starts doing things, listening to things, and behaving in a way that silences her conscience.

Before long there is a searing process in that conscience. The little voice that once cried out is no longer so loud. It is fading now; it is becoming hardened because it has been violated. It makes no difference what other people think now. It is only "what I want to do and what I think" that matters now.

What we see happening on the outside is only evidence of what has happened on the inside. That little girl is no longer able to feel like she once did.

> *This is the first generation of Christians that will dress so immodestly yet still dare to call themselves Christian.*

If you are a Christian, God has a high, holy standard for you. If you are a Christian, you do not take your standard from the world. If you are a Christian, you are not to dress immodestly and lose your blush.

If you are a Christian young lady, your appearance should clearly identify you as a lady. If you are a Christian gentleman, you should not be wearing ponytails and earrings. You should look like a man. If you are a Christian, people should be able to see you at a distance and be able to say, "That is a man" or "That is a woman." If you are dressed like a man, ladies, they cannot tell that. If you are a Christian, you should follow the standards of modesty and identity.

> *What we see happening on the outside is only evidence of what has happened on the inside.*

We are living in a world that is filled with many people who are lost without Christ. According to the Bible, they are on their way to hell, to the blackness of darkness forever. We need to love them and care about them. They are welcome in our churches. We want to preach the gospel to them and bring them to Christ. We want to lovingly plead with them to trust Christ as Savior. We must be people of compassion, but we lose all influence when we become just like the world.

May the Lord help us as Christians to keep God's standards of modesty and identity in our lives.

WHAT IS THE IMPORTANCE OF MODESTY AND IDENTITY?

BIBLE MEMORY VERSES

"So God created man in his own image, in the image of God created he him; male and female created he them."

Genesis 1:27

"The woman shall not wear that which pertaineth unto a man, neither shall a man put on a woman's garment: for all that do so are abomination unto the LORD thy God."

Deuteronomy 22:5

"And let the beauty of the LORD our God be upon us: and establish thou the work of our hands upon us; yea, the work of our hands establish thou it."

Psalm 90:17

"Were they ashamed when they had committed abomination? nay, they were not at all ashamed, neither could they blush: therefore they shall fall among them that fall: at the time that I visit them they shall be cast down, saith the LORD. Thus saith the LORD, Stand ye in the ways, and see, and ask for the old paths, where is the good way, and walk therein, and ye shall find rest for your souls. But they said, We will not walk therein."

Jeremiah 6:15-16

"I will therefore that men pray every where, lifting up holy hands, without wrath and doubting. In like manner also, that women adorn themselves in modest apparel, with shamefacedness and sobriety; not with broided hair, or gold, or pearls, or costly array; but (which becometh women professing godliness) with good works."

I Timothy 2:8-9

"Whose adorning let it not be that outward adorning of plaiting the hair, and of wearing of gold, or of putting on of apparel; but let it be the hidden man of the heart, in that which is not corruptible, even the ornament of a meek and quiet spirit, which is in the sight of God of great price."

I Peter 3:3-4

Chapter Eleven

WHAT DOES GOD'S WORD SAY ABOUT GAY RIGHTS?

 hrough my years of ministry I have dealt with numbers of families who have been affected by the sin of homosexuality.

To hear someone weeping, praying, and asking God for help in this matter changes one's perspective on things. It helps deal with the emotion of anger. The anger is baptized in compassion for hurting people. There are so many hurting people, but we cannot allow emotion for their hurt to cause us to err from the truth.

What does God's Word say about gay rights? The first mention in the Bible of this particular subject is found in Genesis 13:13, speaking of the men of Sodom and their sin. We find in this story of Lot's backsliding that he pitched his tent toward Sodom. The Bible says, *"But the men of Sodom were wicked and sinners before the LORD exceedingly."*

In the nineteenth chapter of the book of Genesis, we find that God rained fire and brimstone from heaven and consumed the cities of Sodom and Gomorrah. As we read this account, we find that these cities were filled with people who were guilty of the awful sin of homosexuality and God destroyed them.

The Bible says in Genesis 19:24-25, *"Then the LORD rained upon Sodom and upon Gomorrah brimstone and fire from the LORD out of heaven; and he overthrew those cities, and all the plain, and all the inhabitants of the cities, and that which grew upon the ground."*

> *There is nothing like the joy that comes from a beautiful Christian home. Anything which perverts God's plan for the home is not right.*

There is nothing as beautiful in this world as a Christian home. I love the church. I enjoy being with the people in the church and serving the Lord in the local church, but we must not forget the beauty of a Christian home.

God has designed the home to have a husband, wife, and children. There is nothing like the joy that comes from a beautiful Christian home. Anything which perverts God's plan for the home is not right.

Many refuse to call sin what it is–sin. The Bible says in Leviticus 18:22, *"Thou shalt not lie with mankind, as with womankind: it is abomination."* God says it is an *"abomination"*! An abomination is the lowest order of sinful behavior.

Let me tell you something that should not only frighten you but should also stir your heart. Our country is being conditioned

and programmed to accept this "lifestyle" and actually promote it as legitimate. The propagation and indoctrination that is being given by activists through educational groups and other civic organizations to condition the thinking of people is alarming.

Consider what has been passed into law in the state of California. According to an August 31, 2002, article in *WORLD* magazine, it is now state law that:

> All K-12 schoolchildren must be taught to 'appreciate' various sexual orientations. Public school teachers and counselors must identify children with the potential to be 'intolerant' of homosexuality–and refer them for retraining. School sports teams that object to homosexual or transsexual behavior may be barred from participating in California Interscholastic Federation sports. All taxpayers must fund marriage-equivalent benefits for homosexual partners of state employees. Nonprofit groups such as the Boy Scouts that refuse to hire homosexuals may be fined up to $150,000 per incident. A person's 'gender' is whatever he or she says it is, regardless of biology.

A man by the name of Swift, who calls himself a homosexual activist, wrote this in *The Gay Community News* a few years ago:

> We shall seduce your sons, emblems of your feeble masculinity, emblems of your shallowed dreams and vulgar lies. We shall seduce them in your schools, in your dormitories, in your gymnasiums, in your locker rooms, in your sports arenas, in your seminaries, in your youth groups, in your movie theaters, in your army bunkhouses, in your truck stops, in your all-male

clubs, in your houses of Congress, wherever men are with men together we shall seduce your sons. Your sons shall become what we want them to become. At our bidding they shall be recast in our image. They will come to crave and adore us.

Young children in public school classrooms are told that they should be conscious and caring about the problems of the world. This sounds innocent enough. Next, they are told that one of the problems of the world is overpopulation and that "alternative lifestyles" should be considered to alleviate this problem. Eventually, they hear that the gay and lesbian lifestyle, if practiced faithfully, could make a tremendous difference with this problem of overpopulation. If the homosexual couple some day wants children, they can simply find a surrogate mother. If the lesbian couple wants a child, they can choose the donor they desire. Something has happened to dull our senses in America. We are getting used to the dark.

I remember reading a lecture given by the well-known television personality, Ted Koppel. He gave the lecture at a Duke University commencement exercise. You can write Mr. Koppel, the news network, or Duke University and ask for a transcript of his speech.

Although he is a Jew, in his speech he sounded like a Baptist preacher. I am not endorsing Ted Koppel, but I want to tell you what he had the courage to say. He spoke to the graduates on the Ten Commandments saying, "We have actually convinced ourselves that slogans will save us. For instance, 'Shoot up if you must, but use a clean needle.' 'Enjoy sex whenever and with whomever you wish, but make sure to protect yourself.'"

He went on to say,

> The answer is 'no.' No! Not 'no' because it is
> cool. Not 'no' because it is smart. Not 'no'
> because you might end up in jail or dying of
> AIDS, but 'no' because it is wrong to live like
> that. I caution you, as one who performs daily on
> that flickering altar of the television, to set your
> sights beyond what you can see. There is true
> majesty in the concept of an unseen power which
> can neither be measured or weighed. There is
> harmony and inner peace to be found in
> following a moral compass that points in the
> same direction, regardless of fashion or trend.

Of course, our God is more than some "unseen power," but
the man makes his point.

There are things that God's Word says are right and things
that God's Word says are wrong. We need to line up our lives
with God's fixed point of reference–the Word of God.

The truth is, we have that moral compass. It is the eternal
Word of God. What the Bible says today about homosexuality
is right, and we need to live by it. We need Bible-believing
Christians who love the Word of God and will live by the
standards of the Word of God.

In all of my reading and research on a number of issues–the
AIDS epidemic, the sin of sodomy, and the homosexual
lifestyle–I could bring many articles to your attention. I could
tell you of descriptive things concerning crimes committed that
would make you nauseated. I have chosen not to do that, but to
share with you the Word of God, and what God says about so-
called rights.

I realize that we live in a pluralistic society. I realize, also, that there is no such thing as absolute freedom. Absolute freedom would mean anarchy. People are saying that the homosexual simply needs love. What that person needs more than love is truth. The Bible says in John 8:32, *"And ye shall know the truth, and the truth shall make you free."* The truth will set him free.

> *We need to line up our lives with the Word of God–God's fixed point of reference.*

In a church like the church I pastor, everyone is welcome. I often think when I am preaching that I am preaching to parents whose children are caught up in what the world calls an "alternative lifestyle," what God calls *"vile affection"* and an *"abomination."* I often think about how heartbroken they are.

Not long ago, I spoke with a mother who has served the Lord for more than forty-one years and has a son in his thirties. By her description, he is a "flaming homosexual." She wept over the phone. She cried as she talked about the bondage that her son is in and how he needs deliverance.

It is the truth that sets people free. No matter what the sin, it brings bondage. Sin comes to us and says, "I will serve you." It might be some habit you have. It may be any number of things, but as we address this particular sin, we must understand that sin is bondage. To be delivered from bondage, God says that the truth will make you free.

THEIR LIES

The Word of God speaks very clearly about the issue of homosexuality in the first chapter of the book of Romans. The Bible says in Romans 1:24-25,

> *Wherefore God also gave them up to uncleanness through the lusts of their own hearts, to dishonour their own bodies between themselves: who changed the truth of God into a lie, and worshipped and served the creature more than the Creator, who is blessed for ever. Amen.*

Notice the Bible says, *"Who changed the truth of God into a lie."* There are many lies associated with the homosexual lifestyle. Let us mention just a few of them.

"THIS IS A CIVIL RIGHTS ISSUE."

This is the only so-called "civil rights" issue that concerns a lifestyle. Thinking people realize that you cannot equate this with the civil rights of minorities or racial groups. Homosexuality is a lifestyle, not a nationality or a race.

When we bend the laws of our country to accommodate the rights of a minority to live a certain lifestyle, we jeopardize all the rights of the majority. The rights that they want are rights without responsibility. There is no freedom like that.

It is not a civil rights issue; it is a sinful lifestyle issue. Remember that John 8:32 says, *"And ye shall know the truth, and the truth shall make you free."*

"PEOPLE ARE BORN THIS WAY."

There is no scientific research or researcher in the world who is willing to admit that people are born homosexuals. People have all kinds of arguments concerning this, but God identifies it as a sin and as a matter of choice.

I have done much reading on the subject of AIDS. I am convinced that this one disease is going to change the way our country functions. It will change all the medical policies of our nation. It will change the food service industry in America and around the world.

The rights that they want are rights without responsibility. There is no freedom like that.

I found in my research that homosexuals account for well over fifty percent of AIDS cases in the United States. This is considerably high when you realize that they make up only one to two percent of the population. We want to do everything we can to eliminate this disease. Does it make any sense that while there is so much publicity about eliminating AIDS as a disease, on the other side of the coin, there is so much promoting of homosexuality as a lifestyle? It does not make sense.

It makes no sense that when America is dying and a catastrophic disease is running rampant across our nation, that we celebrate the lifestyle that is largely responsible for propagating this disease. It is senseless. It is a lie to say that people are born homosexuals.

"THIS LIFE-STYLE IS GAY."

It is another lie to use the slang term "gay" to describe this. A nice word has been forever distorted in the English vocabulary. This way of living is anything but gay.

I have been in the AIDS wards of hospitals. I have seen people who have destroyed their bodies, who clamor for another sex act, while nearly bleeding to death. They are so bound by the bondage of this sin. They live and die in the loneliness of this lifestyle, and then refer to themselves as "gays."

According to some of the articles I have read, those who have done a great deal of research on the subject of suicide believe that as many as fifty percent of the people who commit suicide in this country either have some contact with, or they are practicing homosexuals.

The only way for this lifestyle to continue is by recruitment.

It is not a "gay" lifestyle. It is a lifestyle of bondage. The Bible says that the truth will make you free. *"And ye shall know the truth, and the truth shall make you free."*

"WE WANT TO BE LEFT ALONE."

Another lie that is told by the homosexual community is "We want to be left alone to live our own lives." What I am about to say may sound humorous, but I do not mean for it to be funny. It is not humorous to find out that there may be someone in your family bound by this sin.

These people do not want to be left alone. They cannot be. It is impossible for two people of the same sex, whether they are men or women, to populate the human race. The only way for this lifestyle to continue is by recruitment. I am sure there are some practicing homosexuals who would say that they do not get involved in recruiting others into this sinful, homosexual lifestyle. The truth is that it continues through the process of recruitment.

"TOLERANCE IS THE GOAL."

Homosexual activists claim that they want to promote "tolerance" and "diversity" in our schools and in society. This, too, is a lie.

In some school systems across America, teachers are required to attend sessions for "sensitivity training." Activists say that the only way we can have "safe schools" for students who are "sexually diverse" is to educate teachers and students to be "tolerant" of the homosexual lifestyle. Even lower grade elementary teachers are instructed to use the words *gay*, *lesbian*, and *transgender* as often as possible and to use them in a positive way.

> *Their real goal is to indoctrinate a generation to believe that homosexuality is a normal, acceptable lifestyle.*

In truth, tolerance is not the goal. In fact, preventing "hate crimes" is not the goal either. Their real goal is to indoctrinate a generation to believe that homosexuality is a normal, acceptable lifestyle. They are changing the truth of God into a lie.

A Pentecostal preacher by the name of David Wilkerson, wrote in one of his books, *Parents on Trial,* "Without a doubt, the greatest threat that homosexuals impose on our society is the seduction of our children." He was not speaking only of the seduction into a sex act, but the seduction of our children into accepting a lifestyle. We need to be wide awake and thoughtful about such a thing.

You can see that we have taken the edge off what God calls sin when a generation of Americans asks, "What difference does it make? Let them live their own lives." Man left to himself will destroy himself.

We need to know what God says about gay rights. We need to be acquainted with the lies told by the people practicing this sin.

THE LOWEST LEVEL OF HUMAN DEPRAVITY

This lifestyle is the lowest level of human depravity. Someone might ask, "Are you calling these people the lowest element in society?" The Bible says in Leviticus 18:22 that this lifestyle is an *"abomination."* This means that it is the lowest level of human depravity.

This lesson is not intended to bash the people who call themselves homosexual. It is intended to show you what the Bible says. Excuse the expression, but we should stop using words like *queer.* We should use the very language of the Bible. God calls it *sodomy.* God says they are *"sodomites"* (I Kings 15:12). God says in Romans 1:26 that it is *"vile affection,"* and He says in Leviticus 18:22 that it is an *"abomination."* The strong, clear language of the Bible is the language we should use.

I would to God that everyone who is a practicing homosexual could read this because it is the truth that will set him free. In Romans chapter one, our Lord gives a description of an immoral world, a world that is not evolving, getting better and better, but is degrading, getting worse and worse. The Bible says in Romans 1:21-24,

> *Because that, when they knew God, they glorified him not as God, neither were thankful; but became vain in their imaginations, and their*

foolish heart was darkened. Professing themselves to be wise, they became fools, and changed the glory of the uncorruptible God into an image made like to corruptible man, and to birds, and four footed beasts, and creeping things. Wherefore God also gave them up to uncleanness, through the lusts of their own hearts, to dishonor their own bodies between themselves.

God calls the sinful behavior of these men with men and women with women a dishonor to their own bodies. The Bible continues in verses twenty-six and twenty-seven,

For this cause God gave them up unto vile affections: for even their women did change the natural use into that which is against nature: and likewise also the men, leaving the natural use of the woman, burned in their lust one toward another; men with men working that which is unseemly, and receiving in themselves that recompence of their error which was meet.

This lesson is not intended to bash the people who call themselves homosexual.

When the Lord lists the sins of this degrading, immoral society, He places at the lowest level this lustfulness that men have for men and women for women. God places the sin of sodomy at the lowest level of human depravity. No wonder we are suffering so in our country because of this sin.

You can find details through your own reading and research about the behavior of these people and the length to which they will go in practicing their sin. There are stories about the

depravity of this lifestyle that would be so disturbing that most people could not bear to hear it.

The most popular rock concert tour in America a few years ago was a group in which all the band members were female. *USA Today* reports that over half of those in their audiences are lesbian and homosexual. In the same article, the paper reported that many mothers took their daughters to hear these bands in order to give them their first rock concert experience. Of course, these mothers introduced their daughters to much more than rock music.

This is not an alternative lifestyle. I remind you that, according to the Word of God, it is vile affection and an abomination. The Disney Corporation once reported that nearly forty percent of their employees are practicing homosexuals and lesbians. It is no wonder that in one of their subsidiary companies, Hyperion, they promote books on the homosexual lifestyle for young people to read. The rock singer Elton John, a well-known homosexual, was the featured singer in Disney's highly successful film, *The Lion King*, introducing millions of children to this rock performer and his radical agenda.

> *God places the sin of sodomy at the lowest level of human depravity.*

THE LAST DAYS

The Word of God says in II Timothy 3:1, *"This know also, that in the last days perilous times shall come."* Of course, the term *"last days"* deals with the period of time from the resurrection of Christ to the Rapture of the church.

To many I may sound like an alarmist. Perhaps you think that I have gone to extremes. The Bible says that *"in the last days perilous times shall come."* We have looked at their lies. We have looked at the lowest level of human depravity. Let us look at the last days.

This passage continues in verse two, *"For men shall be lovers of their own selves, covetous, boasters, proud, blasphemers, disobedient to parents, unthankful, unholy."*

When men begin to feel this way about God and about others, the Bible describes them in verse three as, *"without natural affection."*

It is natural for a man to be attracted to a woman. It is natural for a woman to be attracted to a man. God placed us on this earth, and He made the beautiful fulfilling gift of marriage, the union of a man and woman, as a way to populate the earth.

In this lifestyle in the last days, there is an unnatural affection. It is unnatural for a man to lust after another man. It is unnatural for a woman to lust after another woman. It is a perversion of the truth. It is sinful.

People say, "Well, I know some Christians that are this way." The Bible says in I Corinthians 6:9-10,

> *Know ye not that the unrighteous shall not inherit the kingdom of God? Be not deceived: neither fornicators, nor idolaters, nor adulterers, nor effeminate, nor abusers of themselves with mankind, nor thieves, nor covetous, nor drunkards, nor revilers, nor extortioners, shall inherit the kingdom of God.*

According to Scripture, the people in Corinth who were involved in these things were doing this before their salvation. When using the term *"effeminate,"* the Bible says, *"Such were*

some of you." I do not believe that a man or woman can practice this lifestyle and be saved. I believe that people can be led, can be seduced, and can sin; but I have a hard time believing that someone could be a practitioner of this lifestyle and be a genuine Christian.

The Word of God says in verse eleven, *"And such were some of you: but ye are washed, but ye are sanctified, but ye are justified in the name of the Lord Jesus, and by the Spirit of our God."* According to this passage of Scripture, the Lord can deliver someone from this wicked lifestyle.

Living in these last days, what are we to do? The Bible says in Jude 7, *"Even as Sodom and Gomorrah, and the cities about them in like manner, giving themselves over to fornication, and going after strange flesh, are set forth for an example, suffering the vengeance of eternal fire."* God says that this lifestyle is sin. The vengeance of the eternal fire of God is where this lifestyle leads.

Reveal Your True Identity

What are we to do? The Bible says in Jude 3,

> *Beloved, when I gave all diligence to write unto you of the common salvation, it was needful for me to write unto you, and exhort you that ye should earnestly contend for the faith which was once delivered unto the saints."*

What are we to do? In light of all that is going on, how are we to live? We must reveal our identity. The homosexual says that he is "coming out of the closet." He is going to march in a parade. He wants the world to know that he is gay. The shame is that many Christians are still in the "closet" concerning their faith in Christ. People where you work need to know that you are a Christian. They need to know that you love Jesus Christ.

We must speak up, but we must do it compassionately. Do it as though you were speaking to a family member whom you love dearly. Reveal your true identity.

Recruit Others

If they can recruit, we should be recruiting. We should be recruiting people to follow Jesus Christ. They are out recruiting boys and girls, men and women, and young people. They are inviting them to parties, making contacts, trying to convince people in some period of depression that this will bring them joy or happiness, that this is what they have been seeking. We need to be aware of the great recruitment going on by the homosexual community.

We need to rise up as children of God and do our own recruiting for the cause of Jesus Christ. Get busy and tell people about the Lord and tell them how to be saved. Challenge the saved to live like Christians.

In these last days, no one should have to beg you to be faithful to church, read your Bible, or witness to the lost. No one should have to beg you to live decently in this crucial hour of human history. May God help every one of us to be involved in recruiting people to follow Jesus Christ!

Refuse to Compromise Your Biblical Convictions

We should refuse to compromise our biblical convictions. As long as I live, I must speak out against sin. Our children are not growing up in the same America in which we grew up. Their vocabulary is nothing like our vocabulary when we were growing up. Their vocabulary has to do with disease prevention, sexual contact, AIDS, homosexuals, gays, divorce. Things spoken of openly now were things not even mentioned in

private when we were growing up. These precious young people are not growing up in the same America in which we grew up.

We have not come a long way; we have fallen a great distance. The truth is, people need the courage to stand up and say, "The Bible says it is sin, and I don't want to have anything to do with it."

We have not come a long way; we have fallen a great distance.

It is easy to talk like this in church. What about talking like this at work or in your school? Do not come across like you are holier than others. Simply tell people what the Bible says is true.

This lifestyle is anti-God. It is against everything God intended for man. It is a perversion of everything in the Bible pertaining to the home and the family. It can only lead to misery and destruction. The idolatry of our nation has led us to this immoral lifestyle. In our country, it is not only tolerated, it is accepted and promoted. Our only hope is revival. The Lord Jesus can deliver people from this vile affection and set them free.

Are you a Christian? People should know it. We need to reveal our identity. We need to recruit people to follow the Lord Jesus. We need to refuse to compromise the biblically-based convictions by which we live.

WHAT DOES GOD'S WORD SAY ABOUT GAY RIGHTS?

BIBLE MEMORY VERSES

"So God created man in his own image, in the image of God created he him; male and female created he them."

Genesis 1:27

"Thou shalt not lie with mankind, as with womankind: it is abomination."

Leviticus 18:22

"But from the beginning of the creation God made them male and female. For this cause shall a man leave his father and mother, and cleave to his wife; and they twain shall be one flesh: so then they are no more twain, but one flesh."

Mark 10:6-8

"Because that, when they knew God, they glorified him not as God, neither were thankful; but became vain in their imaginations, and their foolish heart was darkened. Professing themselves to be wise, they became fools, and changed the glory of the uncorruptible God into an image made like to corruptible man, and to birds, and fourfooted beasts, and creeping things. Wherefore God also gave them up to uncleanness through the lusts of their own hearts, to dishonour their own bodies between themselves: who changed the truth of God into a lie, and worshipped and served the creature more than the Creator, who is blessed for ever. Amen. For this cause God gave them up unto vile affections: for even their women did change the natural use into that which is against nature: and likewise also the men, leaving the natural use of the woman, burned in their lust one toward another; men with men working that which is unseemly,

and receiving in themselves that recompence of their error which was meet."

Romans 1:21-27

"Know ye not that the unrighteous shall not inherit the kingdom of God? Be not deceived: neither fornicators, nor idolaters, nor adulterers, nor effeminate, nor abusers of themselves with mankind, nor thieves, nor covetous, nor drunkards, nor revilers, nor extortioners, shall inherit the kingdom of God. And such were some of you: but ye are washed, but ye are sanctified, but ye are justified in the name of the Lord Jesus, and by the Spirit of our God."

I Corinthians 6:9-11

"This know also, that in the last days perilous times shall come. For men shall be lovers of their own selves, covetous, boasters, proud, blasphemers, disobedient to parents, unthankful, unholy, without natural affection, trucebreakers, false accusers, incontinent, fierce, despisers of those that are good, traitors, heady, highminded, lovers of pleasures more than lovers of God; having a form of godliness, but denying the power thereof: from such turn away."

II Timothy 3:1-5

Chapter Twelve

WHAT IS TRUE WORSHIP?

od and God alone is worthy of our worship. The Bible tells us that the Lord Jesus Christ traveled through the land of Samaria and met a woman at the well. We read the story in John 4:1-26,

When therefore the Lord knew how the Pharisees had heard that Jesus made and baptized more disciples than John, (though Jesus himself baptized not, but his disciples,) he left Judæa, and departed again into Galilee. And he must needs go through Samaria. Then cometh he to a city of Samaria, which is called Sychar, near to the parcel of ground that Jacob gave to his son Joseph. Now Jacob's well was there. Jesus therefore, being wearied with his journey, sat thus on the well: and it was about the sixth hour. There cometh a woman of Samaria to draw water: Jesus saith unto her, Give me to drink. (For his disciples were gone away unto the city to buy meat.) Then saith the woman of Samaria unto him, How is it that thou, being a Jew, askest drink of me, which am a woman of Samaria? for the Jews have no dealings with the Samaritans. Jesus answered and said unto her, If thou knewest the gift of God, and who it is that saith to thee, Give me to drink; thou wouldest have asked of him, and he would have given thee living water. The woman saith unto him, Sir, thou hast nothing to draw with, and the well is deep: from whence then hast thou that living water? Art thou greater than our father Jacob, which gave us the well, and drank thereof himself, and his children, and his cattle? Jesus answered and said unto her, Whosoever drinketh of this water shall thirst again: but whosoever drinketh of the water that I shall give him shall never thirst; but the water that I shall give him shall be in him a well of water springing up into everlasting life. The woman saith unto him, Sir, give me this water, that I thirst not, neither come hither to draw. Jesus saith unto her, Go, call thy husband, and come hither. The woman answered and said, I have no husband. Jesus said unto her, Thou hast well said, I have no husband: for thou hast had five husbands; and he whom thou now hast is not thy husband: in that saidst thou truly. The woman saith unto him, Sir, I perceive that thou art a prophet. Our fathers worshipped in this mountain; and ye say, that in Jerusalem is the

*place where men ought to worship. Jesus saith
unto her, Woman believe me, the hour cometh,
when ye shall neither in this mountain, nor yet at
Jerusalem, worship the Father. Ye worship ye
know not what: we know what we worship: for
salvation is of the Jews. But the hour cometh, and
now is, when the true worshippers shall worship
the Father in spirit and in truth: for the Father
seeketh such to worship him. God is a Spirit: and
they that worship him must worship him in spirit
and in truth. The woman saith unto him, I know
that Messias cometh, which is called Christ:
when he is come, he will tell us all things. Jesus
saith unto her, I that speak unto thee am he.*

In this particular story, many fascinating things call for our attention. Our Lord said when speaking to this woman in verse twenty-three, but *"the hour cometh, and now is, when the true worshippers shall worship the Father in spirit and in truth: for the Father seeketh such to worship him."* Take note of the expression, *"true worshippers."* I sincerely desire to be a true worshipper of the living God. It is my desire that you be a true worshipper of the Lord Jesus Christ also.

Are you a true worshipper of the Lord Jesus Christ? So much is taking place in many churches in the name of worship that is not true worship. What is true worship? If people go to the church house and they have a Bible and some of the words of their songs seem to be religious words, does that mean they are having worship?

Let me be the first to agree with you if you would like to make the point that we do not have to come collectively and corporately together to worship the Lord. We do worship God alone in our hearts, adoring Him, praising Him, and entering into His presence.

However, we set aside a place to meet, and we normally call it a church building. We come together on the Lord's Day to have what we refer to as *worship*. We indicate by our conversation that we are there to worship the Lord. I think all of us know that the activities that take place in many buildings called "church buildings" are far from true worship.

So much is taking place in many churches in the name of worship that is not true worship.

God has made us so that we might be able to worship Him once we have been redeemed by His precious blood. As a matter of fact, God has designed us to be worshippers of the true and living God. It is impossible for us to be the followers of the Lord that we should be unless we are worshippers of the true and living God.

GOD THE SON SEEKS

We have a God who seeks after us. The Bible says of the Lord Jesus, *"He must needs go through Samaria."* As He came to the well, this woman came at noonday to draw water. She came at noonday because she did not want to be seen. She was a woman who was living in adultery. She previously had five husbands, and she was living with a man who was not her husband. She was the outcast of the city. She did not want to be around other people because they knew what kind of woman she was.

Despite the Samaritan woman's wicked past, she had a divine appointment. She did not know it, but she had an appointment to meet the Son of God at this well because Jesus Christ was going to win her to Himself. He sought her.

Notice a part of this conversation. The Bible says in verses seven through ten,

> *There cometh a woman of Samaria to draw water: Jesus saith unto her, Give me to drink. (For his disciples were gone away unto the city to buy meat.) Then saith the woman of Samaria to him, How is it that thou, being a Jew, askest drink of me, which am a woman of Samaria? for the Jews have no dealings with the Samaritans. Jesus answered and said unto her, If thou knewest the gift of God, and who it is that saith to thee, Give me to drink; thou wouldest have asked of him, and he would have given thee living water.*

First, the Lord Jesus said, *"If thou knewest the gift of God..."* The unsaved do not know the gift of God. This verse speaks of salvation through God's Son. It is the work of those who know the Lord to make this gift known to those who do not know the Lord. We are to speak of God's unspeakable gift and tell a lost world, *"For God so loved the world, that he gave his only begotten Son, that whosoever believeth in him should not perish, but have everlasting life"* (John 3:16).

We have been distracted from the great work God has given us to do–to make this gift known. *"For God so loved...that he gave."* The Lord Jesus paid the price for our sins with His own precious blood on the cross.

Second, the Lord Jesus said, "You don't know *'who it is that saith to thee, Give me to drink.'* You do not know the Lord Jesus Christ." Our Lord worked in this conversation to help this woman know the gift of God and know who He is.

As we are witnessing to people, it is our work to dwell on these two things–to help people know what the gift of God is and who Jesus Christ is. He is the eternal God–coequal, coexistent with God the Father and God the Holy Spirit. He offers the gift of salvation to all who will receive Him.

As the conversation continued, Jesus Christ made the Samaritan woman aware of her need. He asked her about her husband. He brought the subject of sin into view. People cannot be saved until they know they need a Savior. People must be aware of their sin and that their sin separates them from God. Every human being is lost in sin, separated from God because of that sin. The wages of sin is death and hell, and the only payment God will accept is the payment of His own dear Son who bled and died for our sins upon the cross. When Christ died, He said, *"It is finished."* He payed our sin debt in full. This is the only payment God will accept–not our good works. The Bible says that your works and my works, though they may be good works in our eyes, are all nothing more than filthy rags in the sight of God (Isaiah 64:6).

> *We have been distracted from the great work God has given us to do–to make this gift known.*

The Lord Jesus sought after this Samaritan woman. He was seeking for her to know the gift of God. He was seeking for her to know who He is.

GOD THE FATHER SEEKS

In John 4:19 we see that this woman wanted to change the subject. She said, *"Sir, I perceive that thou art a prophet."* She began to talk about worship. The conversation continued in verses twenty through twenty-three,

> *Our fathers worshipped in this mountain; and ye say, that in Jerusalem is the place where men ought to worship. Jesus saith unto her, Woman, believe me, the hour cometh, when ye shall neither in this mountain, nor yet at Jerusalem, worship the Father. Ye worship ye know not what: we know what we worship: for salvation is of the Jews. But the hour cometh, and now is, when the true worshippers shall worship the Father in spirit and in truth: for the Father seeketh such to worship him.*

Perhaps we have read this passage so many times in our devotional reading and missed the last expression in the verse. We know from passages like Luke 19:10 that *"the Son of man is come to seek and to save that which was lost."* We often talk about Jesus Christ seeking after sinners as He was seeking after this sinner. He is seeking sinners so that they might know the gift of God and know who He is–that He is the Christ and the only Savior. He is seeking sinners.

God the Father is also seeking those who have been redeemed and born into God's family to worship Him. This is clearly what the Bible says, *"The Father seeketh such to worship him."*

Did you know that only men who are redeemed can worship the Lord? The unsaved cannot worship the Lord. What are the implications of this? Only the redeemed can worship the Lord because it is the activity of the spirit of the redeemed. It is the action of a redeemed group of people to worship the Lord. The Father seeks people to worship Him. They must be redeemed people, or they cannot worship the Lord.

> *Everything we do for God should come out of our worship of God.*

Everything we do *for* God should come out of our worship *of* God. In other words, we should do what we do because of what God has done for us and because of what we know of the Lord. We love, adore, and worship the Lord. Out of our worship of God comes all that we do for the Lord.

You cannot be a true worshipper of the Father unless you have been saved. However, many churches today hold services that are designed to attract the unsaved. Worldly music is brought in and worldly things are done. The whole program of the service is so much like the world that it is what the world is used to hearing and seeing. The people who plan these services get the idea that this is what the unsaved want and that this is what they will respond to. So, they make the church worldly to attract the world and bring the world into the church. They call this a church service. However, a church service is to be a worship service. You cannot worship God unless you have been redeemed. Remember, the church house is only a place for the church to meet. It is not the church.

Yes, we should be seeking the lost and going after the unsaved. We are to go out into the highways and hedges, but I do not believe that we are to make our services worldly in order to bring in all the world. The world cannot worship God. Only the redeemed can worship God.

A.W. Tozer said,

> Pastors and churches in our hectic times are harassed by the temptation to seek size at any cost and to secure by inflation what they cannot gain by legitimate growth. They are greedy for thrills, and since they dare no longer seek them in the theater, they demand to have them brought into the church. A church fed on excitement is no New Testament church at all. The desire for surface stimulation is a sure mark of the fallen nature, the very thing Christ died to deliver us from. Because we are not truly worshippers, we spend a lot of time in the churches just spinning our wheels, burning the gasoline, making a noise but not getting anywhere. Oh, brother or sister, God calls us to worship, but in many instances we are in entertainment, just running a poor second to the theaters.

Philippians 3:3 says, *"For we are the circumcision, which worship God in the spirit, and rejoice in Christ Jesus, and have no confidence in the flesh."* If we understand true worship, we know that the church should not be designed to have a feel-good service, and the music should not be designed to be feel-good music. The Scottish poet Carlyle said, "Let me make a nation's music, and I care not who makes their laws; I will control that nation." There is something very powerful about music and the way it controls people. It works on the emotions. God seeks *"true worshippers,"* and they can only be redeemed people.

Notice carefully the language of the Bible. Not only does God the Son seek, but also God the Father *"seeketh such to worship him."*

GOD THE SPIRIT SEEKS

How does the Holy Spirit seek? If you have trusted Christ as your Savior, you are indwelt by the Holy Spirit. The moment you ask God to forgive your sin and by faith receive Christ as Savior, the Lord Jesus comes to live in you in the Person of the Holy Spirit. You are indwelt forever by the Holy Spirit.

What does God the Spirit do in you? God the Spirit, in the life of the believer, seeks to worship the Lord Jesus and to exalt Christ. This is why the Holy Spirit in us is grieved when we hear something that is not God-honoring. God the Spirit is seeking to adore and worship the Lord Jesus Christ.

"A church fed on excitement is no New Testament church at all."

– A.W. Tozer

John 4:24 says, "God is a Spirit: and they that worship him must worship him in spirit and in truth." This is a must. The Bible says "must worship." There are three "musts" closely gathered in this gospel record. In John 3:7 the Bible says, "Marvel not that I said unto thee, Ye must be born again." In John 3:14 the Bible says, "Even so must the Son of man be lifted up." The third must is found here in John 4:24, "God is a Spirit: and they that worship him must worship him in spirit and in truth." Give great attention to these things.

The Bible tells us in verse twenty-five, *"The woman saith unto him, I know that Messias cometh, which is called Christ: when he is come, he will tell us all things."* In other words, she was opening up her life and was ready to receive Christ. She said, *"I know that Messias cometh."* She was ready to have Christ revealed to her.

We find salvation in verse twenty-six, *"Jesus saith unto her, I that speak unto thee am he."* In other words, the moment she was ready to receive Him, Christ revealed Himself to her. This is the way salvation always comes.

If I am speaking to an unsaved person, I am trying to help him understand the gift of God and who it is that gives this gift. We must talk about who Jesus Christ is and what He promised to do. The moment that person is ready to have Christ revealed to him, then God reveals Himself to that person. In salvation he trusts Christ as Savior, and God makes Himself known to him. This is a work of the Holy Spirit. The Holy Spirit then comes to live in that person. He is redeemed, and now the Spirit of God in him seeks to exalt, adore, and worship the Lord Jesus. This is vital and must be understood to understand worship. This is not worship in soul. This is worship in spirit.

We are not to worship God in our soul. We are to worship God in our spirit.

When God made me, He made me spirit, soul, and body. In my spirit I have a conscience. In the Bible, my spirit is called *"the candle of the Lord"* (Proverbs 20:27). When I trusted Jesus Christ as my Savior, the Lord Jesus came to live in me–in my spirit. This is where God dwells. I must worship God in spirit.

When we speak of music that honors God and is used to worship the Lord, we are not talking about soul music, but rather spirit music. We are not to worship God in our soul. We are to worship God in our spirit.

There are many people who get emotionally worked up in their souls but do not worship God. They may experience a tremendous high, an exuberance and an adrenaline rush.

However, it is not a spiritual high from the Holy Spirit of God. People can be moved, stirred, and led emotionally by music. But the Bible says that we are to worship God in spirit.

> *If we are truly going to worship God, all eyes must be on the Lamb.*

If you want an idea about a true worship service, see Revelation chapter five. God removes the veil and lets us look into heaven and see the Lord worshipped. You should note that in this scene all eyes are on the Lamb. All eyes are not on the angels, the cherubim, the redeemed, the precious stones, the street of gold, or the gates of pearl. All eyes are on the Lamb!

We may have beautiful buildings, but all eyes must be on the Lamb. We may have people that God has gifted with talent, but all eyes must be on the Lamb. If we are truly going to worship God, all eyes must be on the Lamb. Worship is not a performance. We are to minister to the Lord, and all eyes must be on the Lamb if we are going to be true worshippers.

Revelation 5:9-14 tells us,

> *And they sung a new song, saying, Thou art worthy to take the book, and to open the seals thereof: for thou wast slain, and hast redeemed us to God by thy blood out of every kindred, and tongue, and people, and nation; and hast made us unto our God kings and priests: and we shall reign on the earth. And I beheld, and I heard the voice of many angels round about the throne and the beasts and the elders: and the number of them was ten thousand times ten thousand, and thousands of thousands; saying with a loud*

voice, Worthy is the Lamb that was slain to receive power, and riches, and wisdom, and strength, and honour, and glory, and blessing. And every creature which is in heaven, and on the earth, and under the earth, and such as are in the sea, and all that are in them, heard I saying, Blessing, and honour, and glory, and power, be unto him that sitteth upon the throne, and unto the Lamb for ever and ever. And the four beasts said, Amen. And the four and twenty elders fell down and worshipped him that liveth for ever and ever.

In other words, all eyes were on the Lamb of God, the Lord Jesus Christ. Eyes were not on a praise band, a choir, a soloist, or a preacher. All eyes were on Him. This is true worship.

So many people are attending meetings and having religious experiences. Their souls are being moved, but their spirits are starving. The adrenaline is running high and the experience is one of exuberance, but their spirits are starving. God must be worshipped *"in spirit and in truth."*

> *Once the Holy Spirit comes to indwell us, He seeks in us to worship and adore the Lord Jesus Christ.*

God the Son seeks, God the Father seeks, and God the Holy Spirit seeks. Once the Holy Spirit comes to indwell us, He seeks in us to worship and adore the Lord Jesus Christ.

When we come to the church building and gather together, what should be happening? Our worship begins before we ever arrive in the place that has been set aside for worship. By the way, I am happy that we have a place set aside for worship. This is why we do not allow certain things to be done in this place that has been sanctified as a place of worship. It is not a carnival place or a clowning place. It is not a race track or an entertainment center. It is not a stage. Our services are not productions. This is a place that we have built to come together to honor and adore the Lord. It is set apart as a place where God's people meet together to exalt Christ. It is a place where we can be true worshippers of the true and living God, worshipping Him in spirit and in truth. My heart breaks to think of so many places that have traded true worship for some type of theatrical experience that is starving the spirits and lives of those who come to those places.

> *My heart breaks to think of so many places that have traded true worship for some type of theatrical experience that is starving the spirits and lives of those who come to those places.*

In our homes we should be thinking, "We're going to meet with God and God's people." When we arrive, we arrive at a place where certain things are laid aside. Thoughts have been overtaken and yielded to Christ. Conversations that we might have in our business dealings are not to be brought into this place because we come to worship the Lord. As we enter in, we find a seat in this place set aside to worship Him.

There may be noise and commotion for a time while we are finding our seats. However, in a few moments music begins. The music should be worshipful music that exalts Christ. The prelude should never be a rousing, charging music as if we were going out to a ball game. The music should be something that says, "Be still, my soul. We are coming into the presence of

God." The music is not given simply so that people will have the noise of their conversation covered. After a moment of hearing that music, we realize that we are coming together to worship God with reverence. We should bow our unworthy heads before the Lord and begin to pray that God will speak to us and deal with us. We want to be true worshippers.

The people who have a part in leading the worship service do not do it for other people; they do it for God. The choir has prepared for the Lord. Those who lead have prepared for the Lord.

There are thousands of churches across our land that never have a true worship experience because they have been betrayed by preachers who have turned from being preachers to performers.

Not only does the preacher need to be prepared in prayer, but everyone who has a part in the service needs to be prepared in prayer. Any person who has a part in serving and working should have already prayed and entered into communion with God when he takes his particular place in the worship service. All who have come to worship the Lord need to be praying, believing God, trusting in God, leaning on God, and expecting Him to move and work. Do not get the idea that we are to have some dead, quiet, lifeless meeting. No! This meeting is very much alive, not alive with fleshly entertainment, but alive with the Spirit of the living God.

There are thousands of churches across our land that never have a true worship experience because they have been betrayed by preachers who have turned from being preachers to performers.

Some people are no longer singers; they are entertainers. May God help us. A generation has sold out. Let us be true worshippers of the living God.

In my reading, I came across a story about Martin Lloyd Jones, a well-known English preacher who is now in heaven. He has written many books, but his lengthy book on Romans is a classic. After Martin Jones' death, another preacher went to see his widow and said, "We're sure going to miss your husband's preaching."

What we do in public is to no avail if what we are in private is not mighty with God.

Jones' widow replied, "You're going to miss his preaching, but I'm going to miss his praying. He was mightier in prayer than he was in the pulpit."

When I read that, my heart was so smitten with conviction. I know my wife could not say that; but I want her, by God's grace, to be able to say that.

What we do in public is to no avail if what we are in private is not mighty with God. What so many of us need to do is bring the private, secret part of our lives to the feet of Jesus Christ and say, "Lord Jesus, make me right and holy. Bless me here in the private, secret place of my life." Only then will we be true worshippers of the living God.

WHAT IS TRUE WORSHIP?

BIBLE MEMORY VERSES

"But as for me, I will come into thy house in the multitude of thy mercy: and in thy fear will I worship toward thy holy temple."

Psalm 5:7

"Give unto the LORD *the glory due unto his name; worship the* LORD *in the beauty of holiness."*

Psalm 29:2

"O come, let us worship and bow down: let us kneel before the LORD *our maker."*

Psalm 95:6

"O worship the LORD *in the beauty of holiness: fear before him, all the earth."*

Psalm 96:9

"But the hour cometh, and now is, when the true worshippers shall worship the Father in spirit and in truth: for the Father seeketh such to worship him. God is a Spirit: and they that worship him must worship him in spirit and in truth."

John 4:23-24

"For we are the circumcision, which worship God in the spirit, and rejoice in Christ Jesus, and have no confidence in the flesh."

Philippians 3:3

"And I beheld, and I heard the voice of many angels round about the throne and the beasts and the elders: and the number of them was ten thousand times ten thousand, and thousands of thousands; saying with a loud voice, Worthy is the Lamb that was slain to receive power, and riches, and wisdom, and strength, and honour, and glory, and blessing. And every creature which is in heaven, and on the earth, and under the earth, and such as are in the sea, and all that are in them, heard I saying, Blessing, and honour, and glory, and power, be unto him that sitteth upon the throne, and unto the Lamb for ever and ever. And the four beasts said, Amen. And the four and twenty elders fell down and worshipped him that liveth for ever and ever."

Revelation 5:11-14

Chapter Thirteen

CAN WE HAVE REVIVAL?

f Christian people could have only one prayer answered, what should they ask from the Lord? I believe we should pray for revival. When revival comes, everything else we need will follow.

Considering the subject of revival is not presenting some sort of equation that, if followed, will bring about revival. It is more than stating the facts; it is the touch of God, the work of God. May the Lord move us closer to the burden we should have–a burden for God to send revival.

WHAT OTHERS HAVE SAID ABOUT REVIVAL

"If God has visited His people before, He can and will do so again."
– James McQuilkin

231

"A genuine revival without joy in the Lord is as impossible as spring without flowers, or day-dawn without light."
— C.H. Spurgeon

"Revival cannot be organized, but we can set our sails to catch the wind from heaven when God chooses to blow upon His people once again."
— G. Campbell Morgan

"A true revival means nothing less than a revolution, casting out the spirit of worldliness, making God's love triumph in the heart."
— Andrew Murray

"It is not great talents or great learning or great preachers that God needs, but men great in holiness."
— E.M. Bounds

"If the presence of God is in the church, the church will draw the world in. If the presence of God is not in the church, the world will draw the church out."
— Charles Finney

"Revival is the church falling in love with Jesus all over again."
— Vance Havner

"A revival means days of heaven upon earth."
— D. Martyn Lloyd-Jones

"A revived church is the only hope for a dying world."
— Andrew Murray

As we consider the subject of revival, let us look in the Word of God at the message of the prophet Habakkuk. The book of Habakkuk is brief, containing only three chapters, but in it we find many powerful verses that God uses to speak to our hearts.

The prophet Habakkuk said in Habakkuk 3:2, *"I have heard thy speech, and was afraid: O LORD, revive thy work in the midst of the years, in the midst of the years make known; in wrath remember mercy."*

Note the words, *"revive thy work."* Habakkuk was not praying for himself; he was praying for God's glory and honor.

The prophet Habakkuk was living in the land of Judah on the eve of the captivity of his people. The mighty nation of Babylon was about to sweep down upon Judah and carry captive the people to the land of Babylon. This was God's judgment upon Judah.

We know very little about the prophet Habakkuk. His name means "one who embraces." He embraced the Lord. He was a man who got hold of God.

Oh, how we need people today who can get hold of God. Most churches looking for a pastor are looking for someone who can speak well or looks good. But Habakkuk was a man who embraced God. This frightens many people. It is too serious for some.

We want our preachers to be like our politicians. We want them to be able to get along with everyone, to get as many people in as possible, and to form as many coalitions as possible. We want bigger and better, no matter how many times we must disobey the Lord. As long as it

A revival is a new beginning of obedience to God.

works, we think we should try it. We are doing exactly the opposite of what God says we are to do. In truth, we should be preaching God's Word and depending on the Lord to do what only He can do.

Our God desires to send revival. The Lord wants to bless us. Let us do whatever is necessary for God to bless and send revival.

A revival is a new beginning of obedience to God. A revival does not necessarily mean that the church will explode with growth or that the entire nation will be swept with a feeling to live more righteously. But when revival comes, we will know that God has worked, and the Lord will be glorified in it.

FINNEY ON REVIVAL

Years ago, I read the life story of Charles G. Finney. Most people who have studied the history of revival in our nation would say that he was the man most mightily used of God in revival. Finney gave a list of things about revival. Allow me to give Finney's list with my comments following.

- *Become thoroughly dissatisfied with self and with the utter bankruptcy of the human race.*

In reverse of that, we want to see how impressed we can become with self. We think that surely there is something we can do to bring about what needs to be accomplished in our land. To the contrary, Finney said we must realize our utter bankruptcy.

- *Set yourself on having a changed life.*

- *See that God is able.*

The longer we look to the Lord, the more we desire to look to Him and *keep* looking to Him.

- *Do a thorough job of repenting.*

Let each of us say, "God, be thorough with me." Let the Holy Spirit do the searching. Instead of doing the searching ourselves, let God point out to us what our needs are, and confess those needs to God. It is not easy to come clean with God, though we realize that God knows everything.

- *Yield to the Lord.*

All areas of our lives that we hold for ourselves should be given to God. Nothing about us is of value to God until it is crucified, put to death. Our voices cannot be used for God until they are crucified voices. Our musical abilities cannot be used for God until they are crucified. Our abilities to speak, to stand before people, to use the Scriptures, and to carry forth the message is of no avail to God and for God to work until the instrument is crucified. We must yield to the Lord.

- *Read and meditate on God's Word.*

We are in a hurry with everything, including the Bible. We are looking for quick fixes. The Bible is like eating real mashed potatoes; it takes time and effort to get real mashed potatoes. But we want to have instant potatoes to taste exactly like real mashed potatoes. Real mashed potatoes must be peeled, washed, cut, boiled, and creamed. This is different from taking something flaky out of a box and adding water and heat. We must read and meditate on God's Word.

> *The longer we look to the Lord, the more we desire to look to Him and keep looking to Him.*

- *Give time to prayer.*

For those of us who are easily distracted, we should set a time to meet God. I am not talking about a time to pray; I am saying to be in a certain place for a certain time. Go there to pray.

- *Begin to speak to others about the Lord.*

We want to put this point at number one, but Finney says it is number eight. We might be more like Jesus Christ after the other seven steps. Our testimony would certainly be more powerful after doing the other things first.

- *Expect God to revive you.*

Place faith in God for revival.

PRINCIPLES OF REVIVAL

Let me share with you another list. This list is from a book entitled, *The Awakening That Must Come*. The author states certain principles concerning revival.

- *The principle of the fullness of time*

    A revival awakens a church through the reality that God controls His work and will give His people what they need, when they need it. God is recognized as sovereign. He gives an awakening when His sovereign will pleases. A revival may come quite suddenly and virtually unexpected by the church at large, but God orders all the details. He is the Lord of the harvest.

- *The principle of the emergence of the prophet*

    Revivals usually produce great leaders. There have been exceptions like the Prayer Revival of 1858-1860 that was largely led by lay people. Still normally one or more significant leaders emerge in the movement. Classic illustrations are George Whitefield and John Wesley in the eighteenth century revival in Britain.

- *The principle of progress in spiritual matters*

    A revival foremost generates new spiritual life as it surges through the church and community.

Evangelism, social action, a new awareness of spirituality, etc., always surface. Spirituality superceding materialism becomes paramount in the law of progress in spiritual matters.

• *The principle of variety*

Every revival is unique. No awakening manifests itself identically in detail to any other movement, even though the same basic principles invariably arise. For example, the Prayer Revival centered on prayer while the Eighteenth Century Awakening revolved around great preaching. The Welsh Revival of 1904-1906 featured singing and testimony.

• *The principle of recoil*

Revivals come to an end. Martin Luther said that 'thirty years constitutes the outer limit of an awakening.' Whether he was invariably right or wrong, the sun sets in every revival.

• *The principle of theology*

Theology changes during revivals, often radically. The church returns to basic, conservative thought. When God touches and there is real heaven-sent revival, there is a return to apostolic simplicity and doctrine.

• *The principle of consistency*

All revivals differ, yet certain vital, spiritual elements always surface in revival.

WHAT GOD'S WORD REVEALS

I have studied every word and every verse of Habakkuk, seeking to know God and His intent in the matter of revival. The prophet Habakkuk, with the destiny of his nation set, with the judgment of God coming upon Judah, knew with certainty that the Babylonians were going to be used as an instrument by God to judge His own people. Let us consider what we find as the prophet prayed for revival.

A MAN WITH A BURDEN

We find a man with a burden. The Bible says in Habakkuk 1:1, *"The burden which Habakkuk the prophet did see."* This was not a burden Habakkuk *had;* it was a burden he *saw.* It is not as if he were carrying a heavy weight around and was about to die under the load. The burden was a desire for God to intervene.

This does away with all religious pep rallies. The Saddleback Community Church in southern California has attracted forty-five thousand pastors worldwide to come and study what they are doing. The pastor has said to these pastors, "We must go into the community. We must find out what the people want. We must give them the kind of music that they are used to listening to. When you come here, it's loud. We turn it up loud. It's rock and it's loud." The pastor said in one of the lectures, "I'm standing here as dressed up as I get, with a pair of cotton pants, a sports shirt, and no socks. The only thing I do differently in the wintertime is put on socks."

Of course this can be done to get a crowd. That pastor has done it, and he has a crowd—a very large crowd. This is no small thing. I do not ever remember reading or hearing of any ministry attracting forty-five thousand pastors to study it. But he is only going to do what men can do. What men do will finally wear down and leave people more empty than they were before.

I am not saying that this man is unsaved. I am not saying that people are not getting saved. That is not the point. At the heart of a ministry that takes this approach, you find man-centered religion. May God bring us to a Christ-centered faith.

Habakkuk was a man with a burden to see God intervene. Our sufficiency is not of ourselves. Unless God intervenes, there is no hope.

A VISION OF A HOLY GOD

In Habakkuk 1:12 Habakkuk said, *"Art thou not from everlasting, O LORD my God, mine Holy One? we shall not die. O LORD, thou hast ordained them for judgment; and, O mighty God, thou hast established them for correction."*

Habakkuk was rehearsing back to God what he knew to be true about the Lord. He declared that his God is the Holy One. He had a vision of a holy God.

Our sufficiency is not of ourselves. Unless God intervenes, there is no hope.

Friends, there are certain things that people will not do or attempt to do in the presence of a holy God. There is a certain kind of music that you would not listen to in the presence of a holy God. There is a certain demeanor that you would not display in the presence of a holy God.

Some may not like the idea of being in the presence of a holy God, but it is a vision of a holy God that we need. God says that He is holy and we are to be holy. We can have every kind of youth movement imaginable, bring in a rock band, talk about

Jesus all we want to, work everyone up to a frenzy, and call it anything we want to call it; but, without the holiness of God, there will be no revival. Our only hope is revival!

In the presence of a holy God, we must come clean. This is the wake up call we need–a vision of a holy God.

A WILLINGNESS TO BE REPROVED

Habakkuk 2:1 says, *"I will stand upon my watch, and set me upon the tower, and will watch to see what he will say unto me, and what I shall answer when I am reproved."* We should say, "Lord, I know I have sinned. Show me where I've sinned."

> *Without the holiness of God, there will be no revival. Our only hope is revival!*

In this book about revival, there is a willingness to be reproved. None of us enjoy being reproved. The dearest friend I have is my wife. I am so eternally grateful to God for the relationship the Lord has given us. I have absolutely no doubt about her love. She can tell me things I need to do in my life to make me more of what I should be for God.

When my wife reproves me, it is difficult, but I thank her. If someone else reproves me, helping me to be more of what Christ desires for me to be, I want to be able, by God's grace, to thank him.

This is far removed from the attitude that we find in most places. But in a real, biblical revival, there is a willingness to be reproved. The prophet said, "God, speak to me and show me where I'm wrong. Reprove me."

FAITH IN GOD

In Habakkuk 2:4 we find faith in God. Notice the context of this faith. *"Behold, his soul which is lifted up is not upright in him: but the just shall live by his faith."* In one part of this verse, the Lord deals with everyone who is not doing what is right. In the other part of this verse, God deals with putting one's faith in Him.

The Lord has designed the Christian life so that if nothing goes the way you expected, you can still put your faith in God. Habakkuk was going to deal with all the things that God was bringing upon Judah and the horror associated with the Babylonian captivity. The only way God's people can make it in a world where people are bent on vengeance and immorality is by faith in God.

If you do not have faith in God, this wicked world will wear you down so that you will be good for nothing. You will be trying to straighten out everything and everyone, or you will be overcome by the wicked. God has not assigned us to straighten out everything in this world. God has assigned us to seek Him, to put our faith in Him.

> *The Lord has designed the Christian life so that if nothing goes the way you expected, you can still put your faith in God.*

Sure, we are concerned about a better world, safer air to breathe, and cleaner water to drink. This is part of being a responsible citizen. But it is far removed from the heart of the matter. We must give our lives to something greater than attempting to make the world a better place from which to go to hell.

As a young man, I was listening to an evangelist and he said something that changed my life. He declared, "If your cherished plans don't come out the way you planned, it has nothing to do with your being a victorious Christian if you'll keep your eyes on Jesus Christ."

> *Evangelism cannot be a substitute for revival.*

I allowed this to become a part of my life. God does not change, and He has designed the Christian life so we can live victoriously by keeping our eyes on Him.

Some of you will be so gravely disappointed with something or someone you love that you will think the light of your life is about to go out. But God has designed the Christian life so that we can keep our faith in Jesus Christ and know that He will see us through. The object is to get us back where we should be, trusting God and God alone.

PRAYER SPECIFICALLY FOR REVIVAL

Habakkuk prayed specifically for revival. It was not a general prayer, but prayer for revival. Praying for revival is praying for God to intercede, to intervene, to work and move for His people.

Evangelism has become, in some places, a substitute for revival. Some folks think they are having revival because they are seeing people saved. If you look at it that way, you may be content to see many people saved in a meeting or through some speaker and never experience real revival. If there is revival, there will be many more people saved as a result of it. Evangelism cannot be a substitute for revival.

Habakkuk prayed specifically for revival. Habakkuk 3:1-2 says, *"A prayer of Habakkuk the prophet upon Shigionoth. O LORD, I have heard thy speech, and was afraid: O LORD, revive thy work."*

A PLEA FOR MERCY

"O LORD, revive thy work in the midst of the years, in the midst of the years make known; in wrath remember mercy."

Habakkuk did not come to God with a bargain saying, "Lord, let's make a deal. If You will, I will." God does not work that way.

God says in II Chronicles 7:14, *"If my people, which are called by my name, shall humble themselves, and pray, and seek my face, and turn from their wicked ways; then will I hear from heaven, and will forgive their sin, and will heal their land."*

God has already made it possible to enter into His presence through the merits of Jesus Christ. We do not come and say, "Lord, after all I've done, after all we want to do..." It is as though some people pray, "We're really interested in our country, but Lord, You don't seem to be." Have you stopped to think that God is much more concerned about our country and our world than we are? God is much more concerned about the lost than we are.

We do not have to convince God. We do not need to say, "Get interested, Lord, in what we're doing." This is not the way to approach the Lord. The only prayer we can make to God is a plea for mercy. Mercy is casting ourselves completely at God's feet.

All of us have the same problem–pride. We are proud of the way we look. We are proud of the way we can speak. We are proud of the way we can get things done. We are proud of our humility. Pride is our problem.

God said to Habakkuk, "It's already done. It's finished. It's in the works. Everything is in motion. The hoofs of the Babylonian horsemen can be heard. They are coming. Your nation is judged. You're going to captivity. For seventy years you are going to be there. It's done."

The prophet prayed, "God be merciful to us."

LIVING IN THE "YET"

Let us consider living in the *"yet."* Everything was going to happen just as God said it would. The Bible says in Habakkuk 3:17-19,

> *Although the fig tree shall not blossom, neither shall fruit be in the vines; the labour of the olive shall fail, and the fields shall yield no meat; the flock shall be cut off from the fold, and there shall be no herd in the stalls: yet I will rejoice in the LORD, I will joy in the God of my salvation. The LORD God is my strength, and he will make my feet like hinds' feet, and he will make me to walk upon mine high places. To the chief singer on my stringed instruments.*

We think it is enough that we say, "Lord, I'm going to pull through somehow. I'm going to hold on. Lord, I know You're going to get me through this. Just squeeze me through." That is not living in the *"yet."* The prophet realized that all of this was going to happen, yet he would *"rejoice in the LORD."*

Our God is a consuming fire. We would be consumed if it were not for the mercies of God. In Luke 18:13, a publican came to the temple, smote himself upon the breast, and said, *"God be merciful to me a sinner."* He was actually saying, "The mercy seat, not the law!"

We must have faith in God, rather than worrying about everything in the world or being overcome by evil. Pray specifically for revival, plead for mercy, and then live in the *"yet"* knowing that the Lord Jesus is enough. *"LORD, revive thy work!"*

CAN WE HAVE REVIVAL?

BIBLE MEMORY VERSES

"If my people, which are called by my name, shall humble themselves, and pray, and seek my face, and turn from their wicked ways; then will I hear from heaven, and will forgive their sin, and will heal their land."

II Chronicles 7:14

"Wilt thou not revive us again: that thy people may rejoice in thee?"

Psalm 85:6

"Turn thou us unto thee, O LORD, and we shall be turned; renew our days as of old."

Lamentations 5:21

"Behold, his soul which is lifted up is not upright in him: but the just shall live by his faith."

Habakkuk 2:4

"A prayer of Habakkuk the prophet upon Shigionoth. O LORD, I have heard thy speech, and was afraid: O LORD, revive thy work in the midst of the years, in the midst of the years make known; in wrath remember mercy."

Habakkuk 3:1-2

Appendix

CHRONOLOGY OF A NEW LIFE

 he life of a baby begins long before he or she is born. Every person begins as a separate single cell; nothing new is added but oxygen and nutrition. If the process is not interrupted, a human being will live about nine months in the mother's uterus and decades outside it. That person has never existed before and will never exist again.

First Month

Fertilization–life begins! The sperm joins the ovum (egg) to form one cell. This one cell contains the complex genetic blueprint for every detail of human development–the child's sex, height, skin tone, eye color, hair color, shoe size, and intelligence are determined at fertilization by the baby's genetic code in the forty-six human chromosomes. The fertilized egg travels down the fallopian tube into the uterus, where the lining has been prepared for implantation. Within two or three hours the cell divides into two new cells. During the first three days it splits into thirty-two cells. By the fifth day it will divide into ninety cells. Within one week of fertilization, a new human being implants in the mother's uterus and is nourished there. The little egg and the tiny sperm are now an embryo. The embryo has three layers of tissue which develop separately. The outer layer grows into the baby's skin and nerves. The middle layer grows into cartilage, bones, connective tissues, muscles, the circulatory system, kidneys, and sex organs. The inner layer grows into the organs of breathing and digestion. At twenty-two days the baby's heart begins to beat. During the third week the spinal cord develops. By the end of the first month, the kidneys, liver, and digestive tract are beginning to form. The baby is about one-half of an inch long, and weighs about one-third of an ounce.

Second Month

At thirty-three days, the baby's fingers and feet begin to develop. At six weeks, the baby has brain waves that can be measured with an electroencephalogram. The end of human life can be defined as the cessation of brain waves, but many ignore the scientific evidence of brain waves in unborn babies. Milk teeth form at six-and-a-half weeks. At seven weeks the unborn baby swims freely in the amniotic sac with a natural swimmer's stroke. By eight weeks all of the baby's body systems are present. At nine weeks, fingerprints are evident and never change. The baby, now a fetus, is about one and one-fourth inches long from head to buttocks and still weighs less than one ounce.

Third Month

During the third month the baby sleeps, awakens, and exercises muscles energetically–turning its head, curling its toes, and opening and closing its mouth. The baby has developed the body parts required to experience pain, including all of the nerves, spinal cord, and thalamus. The palm, when stroked, will make a tight fist. The baby breathes amniotic fluid to help develop the respiratory system. All organ systems are functioning. From this age on, there is only growth in size and maturation of the organs already present. The baby has a skeletal structure, nerves, and circulation. By the end of this month the baby is about four inches long and weighs just a fraction over one ounce.

Fourth Month

By the fourth month the baby, nourished by the placenta, is developing reflexes, such as sucking and swallowing. The bag of water cushions the baby from bumps, keeps it at a constant warm temperature, enables it to exercise its limbs and move freely, and provides liquid for it to practice swallowing. The water inside the bubble of membranes is always fresh as it replenishes itself completely every six hours. The baby's heart pumps the equivalent of twenty-five quarts of blood a day. During the sixteenth week, the baby can grip. The baby is now about six to seven inches long and weighs around five ounces.

Fifth Month

During the fifth month the baby has a real growth spurt. The internal organs are maturing. The baby begins to sleep and wake at regular intervals. Half the pregnancy has now passed, and many babies begin to grow hair during this month. Babies born at this stage of development (nineteen or twenty weeks) have survived. At the end of the month, the baby is about eight to twelve inches long and weighs from one-half to one pound.

Sixth Month

In the sixth month the baby continues to grow rapidly. The organ systems are still developing. The baby's skin is red and very wrinkled, with no underlying fat. The finger and toe prints are visible. The baby's eyes open, and the baby can see the light that filters through Mommy's abdominal wall. At the end of this month, the baby has completed two-thirds of its stay in the womb. The baby is about eleven to fourteen inches long and weigh about one to one-and-a-half pounds.

Seventh Month

The seventh month marks another period of rapid growth for the baby. Calcium is being stored, and fetal bones are hardening. The baby exercises by kicking and stretching. It sucks its thumb, hiccups, and may cry. Four senses are now used: the eyelids open and close, eyes look around, the baby can taste and touch, and the mother's voice is recognized. Fat begins to be deposited and baby starts to really gain weight. The baby is about fifteen inches long and weighs around three pounds.

Eighth Month

The skin begins to thicken with a layer of fat stored underneath for insulation and nourishment. The baby absorbs a gallon of amniotic fluid per day; the fluid is completely replaced every three hours. By the end of this month, the baby is about eighteen inches long and weighs around five to five-and-a-half pounds, almost doubling its weight.

Ninth Month

In the ninth month, the baby's quarters become so cramped that it can only turn from side to side and most babies have now settled into a head-down position. About a week before birth, growth is stopped, and changes in the mother's hormonal balance aids in the onset of labor and birth. At forty weeks the baby will be full term and measure nineteen to twenty-one inches in length and weigh six to nine pounds.

One cell has become two hundred million cells before birth, and these cells weigh six billion times more than the fertilized egg.

This article was used by permission
from Tennessee Right to Life.

Sunday School materials are available for use in conjunction with *Issues of Life Answered From the Bible.* For a complete listing of available materials from Crown Christian Publications, please call 1-877 AT CROWN or write to: P.O. Box 159 ❖ Powell, TN ❖ 37849

Visit us on the Web at FaithfortheFamily.com
"A Website for the Christian Family"

CROWN
CHRISTIAN
PUBLICATIONS
Royal Reading